CREDIT REPAIR FOR MORTGAGE
LOAN APPROVAL

CREDIT REPAIR FOR MORTGAGE LOAN APPROVAL

You handle the easy stuff. Let credit repair companies handle the hard stuff.

M. Joyce Brown

ISBN: 1973749378
ISBN-13: 9781973749370
Library of Congress Control Number: 2017911397
CreateSpace Independent Publishing Platform
North Charleston, South Carolina

To

Jerome V. Brown

1948–2012

*My beloved husband, who believed
in me when I did not believe in myself*

Contents

One day, a young lady, whom I will call Susie, came into my office, needing help purchasing a home. I reviewed Susie's credit report. It contained too many outstanding collections. She did not have the funds to pay them off, and she didn't have enough good payment history to obtain approval for a mortgage loan, which is a loan used to purchase a home. I told her that she could not qualify for a mortgage loan and would not be able to purchase a home. Susie told me that she had paid $3,000 to a credit repair company to help her get approved for a mortgage loan. After the credit repair company took her $3,000, they told her that she did not make enough money to purchase a home because she was employed as a cook at an elementary school cafeteria. Susie told me, "Ms. Brown, all I want is a home with a backyard for my two little boys to play in. It does not have to be anything fancy."

That made me mad because if she had come to me first, I could have helped her get a mortgage loan approved through a lender who would accept a credit score of at least 500. The lender required all outstanding collections to show a zero balance and three trade lines of alternative credit. (Alternative credit is an account that does not appear on a credit report; examples of alternative credit are monthly payments made for rent, utilities, cell phone, cable, insurance, and other accounts for which the borrower can provide documentation of good payment history.) Susie paid all her monthly utilities and rent on time and did not have any late payments in the past two years. Instead of paying $3,000 to the company, Susie could have used $2,000 to pay off her outstanding collections, and the remaining $1,000 could have paid her up-front closing costs to purchase a home. Susie's income qualified her for a grant of $10,000 to help pay her down payment and closing costs. Susie could have been a homeowner if she had not paid the credit repair company $3,000.

My heart went out to Susie because she had given most of her income tax refund to a company that had taken advantage of her because she wanted to achieve the American dream of becoming a homeowner. I was familiar with the company Susie had used and knew that I could not bad-mouth it, but I decided that I could come up with an alternative. I had worked for ten years as a mortgage loan officer and knew what mortgage underwriters needed to see on a credit report to approve a loan. When Susie came into my office, I was the housing officer at the Dallas County Home Loan Counseling Center in Dallas, Texas, and I provided pre-purchase housing counseling to first-time homebuyers. With this experience, I developed the seminar "Do-It-Yourself Credit Repair for Mortgage Loan Approval" and taught the seminar for fourteen years. More than five thousand participants have attended the seminar. Many participants have taken the knowledge they gained and repaired their credit without the help of a credit repair company.

During the fourteen years I taught the credit repair seminar, I still had appointments with clients who had trusted the claims of credit repair companies and found themselves scammed. One client in particular, whom I will call Paula, came to my office because a credit repair company had guaranteed her that it could improve her credit score so she could get a mortgage loan approved. She needed to be out of her current home in ninety days, and the credit repair company assured her there would be no problem getting her approved in a couple of months. After ninety days, Paula was homeless because the credit repair company was not able to deliver on its promise to increase her credit score to qualify for a mortgage loan. When I reviewed Paula's credit report, I saw that it was impossible for her to obtain mortgage loan approval because she had defaulted on school loans and had recent late payments on some accounts.

It is my hope that this book empowers you to believe you can improve your credit without the help of a credit repair company. *Credit Repair for Mortgage Loan Approval* will give you a basic understanding of credit, how to improve your credit score, and how to handle outstanding collections on your credit report. It will also teach you what a mortgage lender reviews when approving your loan. A credit repair company may improve your credit score, but items may remain on your credit report that will prevent you from obtaining mortgage approval.

I will take you step by step through the credit repair process, so you can repair your credit report yourself and receive all the benefits of having a high credit score. I am not against credit repair companies, but I am against credit repair companies that scam their customers. After reading this book, if you do choose to use a credit repair company, you will be able to determine if the company you are working with can deliver on its promises.

Unless you were taught the importance of good credit growing up, you probably did not think about your credit until you were ready to purchase a new car or your first home. Without good credit, you face the reality that the car or home you want to purchase will have to wait until your credit improves. Not sure that you can improve your credit yourself, you start looking for a credit repair company to help you.

Everyone is talking about credit repair. Television commercials, Internet advertisements, billboards, and radio advertisements all claim they can help you erase bad credit so you can get the car or home you always wanted. Most have quotes from satisfied customers who proclaim that their credit scores went up 60 points in a few months, which enabled them to meet their financial goals. After more than twenty years of reviewing credit reports, I can assure you that every credit file is different. What works for one person will not necessarily work for you.

Credit repair is the process of reviewing your credit report to make the changes necessary to increase your credit score so you can obtain approval on credit applications. During the credit repair process provided in this book, you will perform some or all of the following actions, depending on the information contained in your credit file:

1. Dispute inaccurate information with CRAs, creditors, or collection agencies.
2. Pay down credit card balances.

3. Settle outstanding collection accounts.
4. Bring current any accounts showing late payments.
5. Establish new revolving credit accounts.
6. File affidavits and police reports for identity theft.
7. Establish good payment history on credit accounts.

Many credit repair companies will dispute information, even if it's accurate, in hopes that it will be removed or deleted from the credit report. Disputing information this way is like a game of craps; you will get lucky on some and lose on others. If the disputed account is not removed or corrected, the credit reporting agency (CRA) will reference the account as being "in dispute," which may make it difficult for you to obtain approval of your mortgage loan.

The Credit Repair Organizations Act (CROA) was passed in 1996 to protect consumers against unethical credit repair companies. The federal law requires credit repair companies to advertise and communicate with consumers honestly. Credit repair companies cannot promise that they can remove accurate information, nor can they help you set up a new credit file. Make sure the credit repair company you use complies with the federal law.

Credit Repair for Mortgage Loan Approval will focus on disputing only inaccurate information. In the last step, I will explain in detail how to handle accurate delinquent accounts to increase your credit score and get your mortgage loan approved.

In the pages that follow, I will give you seven simple steps to help you improve your credit. Don't skip around. Completing the steps in order will help you improve your credit score as well as provide the information that mortgage lenders need to see on your loan application to approve your loan.

Step 1

CREDIT REPORT

The first thing you must do is obtain a copy of your personal credit report. You cannot repair what you cannot see. The best source to use for this is the Annual Credit Report Request Service. The Fair Credit Reporting Act (FCRA) allows you to obtain a free copy of your credit report from each of the three national credit reporting agencies, Experian, Equifax, and TransUnion, every twelve months.

You can obtain your reports either online, by phone, or by mail through this service. (You will not get a free credit report if you order directly from Experian.com, Equifax.com, or Transunion.com.)

Online: Visit www.annualcreditreport.com—Report received instantly.

By phone: Call 1-877-322-8228—Report received within fifteen days by mail.

By mail: Complete the annual credit report request form and mail to the following address:

Annual Credit Report Request Service
PO Box 105281
Atlanta, GA 30348–5281

Report received within fifteen days of the date of receipt.

If you are not comfortable with computers, I would recommend that you order your credit report by mail or phone. Also, when ordering your credit report online, order one report at a time. When you order one report at a time, you will have to enter your personal information three separate times to get your reports. If you order all three at once, you must click the correct box to receive your reports. If you do not click the correct box, you will be returned to annualcreditreport.com and will have to wait another twelve months before you can receive the free credit report you were requesting.

Credit reports ordered from a mortgage lender, car dealership finance manager, or credit monitoring service may not provide sufficient information to do credit repair. The credit reports you receive from the Annual Credit Report Request Service will provide the date of original delinquency or the date the account will be removed from the credit report. This information will help you determine which delinquent accounts you will need to resolve first to see an improvement in your credit score. Working on resolving recent delinquencies will provide a greater increase in your score than resolving older delinquencies. Since these are your personal credit reports and only you see them, they will include the name of any company placing a medical collection on your credit report. The name is not included on other credit reports because the FCRA limits the disclosure of medical information. For example, you might have a collection from the Cancer Center; if this were included on a credit report an employer could obtain, the medical information might affect the employer's decision to hire you.

When ordering your credit reports online, be prepared to answer verification questions concerning your identity. These questions help prevent you from being a victim of identity theft. Before you begin, have the names of your accounts, dates they were opened, monthly payment amounts, and your old phone numbers handy. Some questions may not apply to you, and if the account is not yours, it is OK to check "none of the above." If you do not answer these questions correctly, you will have to obtain your credit report by mail. Be sure to print the web page showing you did not receive your credit report and include a copy with your mailed request. This will prevent the service from assuming you received a copy of your credit report online and you are not eligible to receive another free report for twelve months. If you move frequently or have not applied for credit in several years, the computer may not be able to locate you with the addresses you supply, and you will probably have to request your credit reports by mail.

If you are not able to order your credit report online, by mail, or through the toll-free phone number, you may have to order it directly from Experian, Equifax, or TransUnion for a fee. If you order by mail, you may be required to provide a copy of a state-issued identification card and a copy of a utility bill showing your current address and provide a previous address to prove your identity.

If you are married, you and your spouse will have separate credit files, and you will have to order your credit reports individually.

You can also obtain a free copy of your credit report if you are denied credit, unemployed, on public assistance, or a victim of identity theft. If denied credit, your denial letter will provide instructions on how to obtain a copy of your credit report.

Make sure you obtain credit reports from Experian, Equifax, and TransUnion, because your lender will review each of these credit reports when you apply for a mortgage loan.

If you have not requested a copy of your credit report or applied for new credit in a while, you may start receiving phone calls from collectors because you have updated the contact information on your credit file.

CREDIT SCORE

Your credit score is a three-digit number that tells a creditor how likely you are to make on-time payments if granted credit. Your credit report from the Annual Credit Report Request Service will not include your credit score. You must order your credit score separately.

You can obtain your credit score from any company or agency at the beginning of the credit repair process, except from a mortgage lender. If you have a low credit score and a mortgage lender pulls your credit report, the inquiry from that pull can raise questions if you decide to apply with a different lender. Also, you may have difficulty negotiating settlements if the creditor or collection agency sees an inquiry from a mortgage lender. An inquiry from a mortgage lender shows that you are trying to purchase a home. The creditor or collection agency will assume you must settle to obtain mortgage loan approval and may require a settlement at a higher amount than you could otherwise have negotiated.

You can obtain your credit score from any of the major CRAs (for a fee), from a credit monitoring service, from credit card companies offering a free credit score on your monthly credit statement, or from companies offering free credit scores on the Internet. I have listed companies offering free credit scores in the resources section of this book. If you are required to provide your credit card number when ordering your credit score, the score is not free. You are probably agreeing to a one-month free trial, after which the credit monitoring service will charge you a monthly fee.

For approximately $60, you can obtain credit scores and credit reports from Experian, Equifax, and TransUnion at www.myfico.com. If you do not have the funds to pay for the credit reports now, you can wait and use this resource later. Make sure you order you credit report from www.myfico.com at least six months before you apply for your mortgage loan, since 90 percent of mortgage lenders use FICO scores. When I provided credit counseling to clients, I did not see much difference between the FICO mortgage score version and the mortgage lender scores. When you order credit scores from www.myfico.com, the first scores to appear are FICO version 8. Click "View additional FICO score versions used in mortgage, auto, and bank card decisions" under the FICO 8 scores. You will go to a new web page showing the different types of FICO scores. Your mortgage credit score for each CRA is the second score on the list entitled "Commonly Used in Mortgage Lending." My mortgage lending score was between 29 and 37 points lower than my FICO 8 score. If I had used the FICO 8 score, I would have been surprised that I could not get the best interest rate when the lender pulled my credit report during the loan application process.

Step 2

Completing a Budget and Establishing an Emergency Fund

What does budgeting have to do with credit repair? Knowing how much money you have coming in and going out will help you make your payments on time. Good payment history accounts for 35 percent of your credit score. In addition to creating a budget, it is important that you start an emergency fund. The emergency fund will give you the extra money you need to handle emergencies, so you won't have to use money that you set aside to pay your monthly expenses. If you are not able to pay your monthly expenses on time, especially credit cards and loans, these late payments will decrease your credit score.

Budgeting is just a matter of looking at the amount of money you receive on a monthly basis and the monthly and periodic expenses you have to pay. In this step, I will provide basic information on budgeting and creating emergency funds. You can find thousands of books and websites providing information on how to budget on the Internet.

Your primary reasons for establishing a budget are

1. to make sure you have enough income to make on-time payments on current accounts reporting to CRAs;
2. to determine if you have surplus income to settle delinquent accounts or pay down outstanding debt on revolving credit accounts;
3. to determine if you have surplus income to obtain a secured credit card if you do not have any revolving credit accounts on your credit report;

5

4. to start saving for the down payment and closing costs necessary to purchase a home; and

5. to know you can afford the mortgage payment calculated by your mortgage loan officer.

HOW TO GET STARTED WITH YOUR BUDGET

First, look at the amount of income you have coming into your household. Reviewing monthly income is usually very simple, since most income is now directly deposited into a checking or savings account or on a prepaid card. The amount deposited is your *net income*, and you are only concerned with the money that you can spend. Don't forget to include other income that you receive by check or cash.

Next, look at your *monthly expenses*. These expenses include your rent or mortgage payment; utility expenses; auto or finance company loan payments; payments for auto, life, and health insurance; and any other expenses you pay every month. Make a list of these expenses and the amount that you pay monthly. If you are using a credit card, don't forget to count these expenses in your budget.

To budget for expenses that vary monthly, such as utilities, total what you paid over the past year, and divide by twelve to get a monthly average. These *variable expenses* can be higher or lower than the average in any given month, so estimate a payment you can easily make without having to rob Peter to pay Paul. Add all these expenses together to come up with your monthly total.

Next, look at your *periodic* or *irregular expenses*. These are expenses paid at different times during the year. Payments can vary annually; every two, three, or four months; or during a season. For example, payment for auto inspections and registrations are usually paid yearly. If you pay for yard service, you probably pay more during the summer months. If you have children in school, you may have a large expense for clothes and supplies at the beginning of each school year and monthly expenses during the rest of the year. Make a list of these expenses, add up the estimated amounts, and divide by twelve to come up with a monthly expense. This is the amount you should set aside each month to pay these expenses when they become due. I like what Mary Hunt, author of the book *Debt-Proof Living*, says: "We have selective amnesia when it comes to these expenses. We do not think about them until they become due." If you have not planned for periodic or irregular expenses, when they become due, you may find yourself using funds you have set aside to pay monthly expenses and may end up making late payments on your credit card and loan accounts.

Finally, you want to determine how much surplus income you will have available to settle collections or obtain a secured credit card. Take your net income and subtract your monthly and periodic expenses to get either a surplus or a shortage. If you have a surplus, then you are at a good starting point. If you have a shortage, then you do not have enough money to meet your monthly expenses. You will need to go back and review your expenses to see if there are any that you can reduce. If you are not able to reduce expenses, you may need to get a part-time job to provide additional income to bring your budget out of the shortage.

Don't forget to include your monthly fun activities in your budget. Include hobbies and things you enjoy doing, such as going to the movies or going out to eat, but reduce the amount you normally spend.

If you completed your budget and it shows that you have a surplus but if you do not have any savings in your bank account, track your spending for one month. Save all your receipts and record those expenses each day. Don't forget to record those trips to the vending machine, pet expenses, and cash paid for children's school expenses. At the end of the month, total your expenses. Also, review your bank statement for other monthly expenses paid by check or debit card. Complete a second budget to help you determine where your money is going.

If you need help establishing your budget, you can contact a counseling agency approved by the Department of Housing and Urban Development (HUD), and a counselor can help you establish your budget at either no cost or for a small fee. Some HUD-approved agencies receive federal funding to provide counseling services. You can locate a counseling agency near you by going to www.hudexchange.info/housing-and-homeless-assistance. A sample budget from the Federal Trade Commission is included in the exhibits section at the end of the book.

Do not skip this step. If you carry your budget in your head, it is now time to put it down on paper to make it real so you can see the numbers. Too many times, we believe we can afford to pay for an item, only to discover later we forget about another account we needed to pay. Numbers never lie. One plus one will always be two.

If you do not already follow a written budget, this may be difficult for you at first. You may forget and purchase items that are not on your budget or items you do not need. Just know that you have developed a habit of spending without following a written budget, and it may take a while for you to change that habit. A study conducted by Phillippa Lally and reported in the *European Journal of Social Psychology* in October 2010 stated that behavior change can take anywhere from 18 to 254 days. Even after a limb is amputated, the brain can still receive signals of pain as if the limb was still there. You will need to allow some time for your brain to adjust to the changes you are making. An attempt to change your behavior is better than never trying. Continue trying, and your brain will eventually catch up with your desire to stop living from paycheck to paycheck.

ESTABLISHING AN EMERGENCY FUND

Everyone should have an emergency fund. Most financial planners will recommend that you have an amount equivalent to three to six months of monthly expenses. If six months' worth of monthly expenses is more than you think you can save, start with one month. If one month's expenses set aside in an emergency fund is not achievable for you at this time, start with whatever you can. Dave Ramsey, radio host and author of *The Total Money Makeover*, recommends starting an emergency fund with $1,000.

I started my emergency fund with $1,000, and for a long time, that is all I had in the bank. However, just that $1,000 helped me manage many emergencies without having to rob Peter to pay Paul. An emergency fund is a key to helping you make on-time payments on your credit accounts, loan accounts, and monthly rent. On-time payments are important in improving your credit score and obtaining approval of your mortgage loan.

Step 3

Reviewing Credit Score and Credit Score Reason Statements

WHAT IS YOUR CREDIT SCORE?

Your credit score is a three-digit number that represents your payment history on the day the score is calculated. Your credit score tells a creditor how likely you are to make on-time payments should the creditor grant you credit. Credit scores range between 300 and 850. A high score indicates you are a good risk and will probably make your payments on time. A low score indicates you are a high risk, and your previous payment history may indicate that you cannot make your payments on time. If you have a low credit score, a lender may decline your credit application; if your application is approved, you may have to pay a higher interest rate or make a larger down payment. Most mortgage lenders require a minimum credit score before your loan application is processed.

Your credit score will determine if you are ready to apply for your mortgage loan. Many companies offer credit scores, and the scoring models used to determine these scores can be very different. A scoring model reviews your credit history to predict your future creditworthiness. These credit scores vary based on the scoring model and can easily be 20 to 30 points higher than the mortgage lender's credit score. Even FICO, the company that developed the credit score, has twenty-eight different scoring models. When you obtain your credit score, look at what scoring model the company uses. The most commonly used scores are FICO 8 and VantageScore 3.

The scoring model used at the beginning of the credit repair process is not important, since a poor score is poor, regardless of the model. Each scoring model will supply you with a list of reasons why your score is low or if your score is high, reasons that can help you improve your score. These reason statements will probably be the same regardless of the scoring model used. (I will review common reason statements later in this chapter.) In this step, we are using the credit score as a starting point to determine if you are ready to make a loan application.

If you think you are ready to apply for the mortgage loan, check your credit scores at www.myfico.com. This site provides the credit scores that lenders use to approve auto loans, mortgage loans, and credit cards. The scores below are based on the versions used by Experian FICO Score 2, TransUnion FICO Score 4, and Equifax FICO Score 5. Lenders will look at all three scores and use the middle score of the three as the qualifying score for your mortgage loan approval. Use the following credit score guidelines to determine if you are ready to make application for a mortgage loan.

Poor:	579 or below
Fair:	580–619
Average:	620–679
Good:	680–739
Very Good:	740–799
Excellent:	800+

If your credit score is 680 or higher, you can probably contact any lender and start your application for a mortgage loan. A credit score of 740 or higher means you can shop lenders to get the best interest rate. If your credit score is between 620 and 679, you can still contact a mortgage lender, but you may be limited in the types of loan products available to you. Work to improve your score to the highest score you can obtain. If you apply for loan application with a minimum score of 620, an unexpected collection account can appear on your credit report during the loan process and decrease your score so you will no longer qualify for the loan.

If your credit score is between 580 and 619, depending on your payment history, you might find a lender to approve your loan, but you may have to make a down payment of more than 3.5 percent. You will also need to have cash in the bank equal to two mortgage payments after you have made your down payment and paid closing costs. Any delinquent or derogatory credit must be the result of circumstances beyond your control, and your credit file must show you have reestablished a good payment history.

If your credit score is 579 or lower, you have much work to do to improve it, and it will probably take a year or more to obtain mortgage loan approval. Don't get discouraged, however, because this book was written to help you reach your goal of homeownership. Just follow each step as outlined.

REASON STATEMENTS

If your credit score is low, take a moment to review the reason statements. Each report will list three or four reasons why your score is low, and you will use these reason statements to determine where to start the credit repair process. The process is easier if you focus on the reason statements, rather than on the actual score. Some credit scores will show these statements as key factors or factors.

Read the first reason statement. If the reason is "Number of accounts with delinquencies," then you will need to work on decreasing the number of delinquencies by negotiating with the creditors or collection agencies to have these accounts removed or to show that they have been paid as agreed. If the reason is "Lack of revolving account information," then you will need to open a revolving credit card account.

After you have finished with the first reason, then move to the next reason. After you have finished the second reason, then move to complete the third reason. Continue this process until you have worked on all your reason statements. The reason statements are listed in order of importance and resolving the first reason will provide a greater increase in your score than resolving the last reason. However, if you are not in a position to resolve the first reason, work on the reasons that you can. Any reason that you are able to resolve will provide an increase in your credit score. There will be some reasons, like "Recent delinquency is too short," for which you will not see an immediate improvement in your credit score. If you had a recent late payment on a credit account, the original lender is not going to erase the late payment because they have an accurate record of your payment history on their books. You will have to continue to pay on-time for six to twelve months before you see any increase in your credit score.

These reason statements point you toward the direction for most important actions you can take to improve your score. I have had clients come into my office wanting to know which collection accounts to pay off when the reason for their low scores was "Proportion of balances to credit limits on revolving accounts is too high." The credit score increases when balances on revolving credit accounts are low. After further review, I discovered that most of the collections accounts were almost seven years old and would soon fall off the credit report, and the outstanding collections were not the reason for the low scores. If the clients had paid the collection accounts, they would not have seen any increase in their scores.

If your reason statement is not listed in the examples below, go to www.ReasonCode. org. Type in the reason statement, and the website will give you information on what you must do to improve your credit score.

Reason statement examples

- Serious delinquency and public record or collection filed
  The above statement will always appear as the first reason on your credit report if you have delinquent or derogatory credit. *Delinquency* is an account that is thirty days or more past due. A *public record* is an account for which the creditor took you to court to collect payment and the court ruled you were obligated to pay the

account. A *collection* is an account that has received no payment for six months or more and was contracted or sold to a third party to collect. If you have delinquent credit and that is the reason you are doing the credit repair, you will ignore this reason for now. Go to the next reason statements listed, which will provide more insight into the specific delinquency reasons causing this statement to be listed.

- Number of accounts with delinquency

    When this appears, it usually means that you have more delinquent accounts than you have accounts showing good payment history. Your credit score will not improve until you can delete some of these accounts from your credit report. You can negotiate a settlement with the creditor or collection agency to have the account deleted. You can also dispute the item and have it removed from your credit report if the CRA has kept the account on the credit report longer than it is allowed by law. Step 7—Dispute, settle, or forget—will guide you through this process.

- Time since derogatory public record or collection is too short

    The above statement will appear when you have missed a payment in the past year. Your credit report may show a thirty-, sixty-, or ninety-day delinquency or an outstanding collection account. If you are missing payments resulting in delinquencies, review your budget. There is no quick fix in this area. You must make on-time payments for six months or longer before you see an increase in your credit score.

    Even if you have the minimum credit score for a mortgage lender to review your loan application, the lender may not approve an application with a late payment within the past twelve months if the credit file shows a history of late or missed payments. The lender may require you to provide an explanation of why the payment was late. An explanation of "I forgot, or "I had to make car repairs" or "I loaned money to my sister, and she did not pay me back" may result in your loan being declined because it shows you cannot responsibly handle your credit obligations. The reason may seem good to you, but it won't to the lender. You should have been able to pay those accounts from your emergency fund before the due dates. The explanation of "I forgot" is not a good excuse because payment on most accounts is easily drafted from your bank account. "I forgot" might be acceptable if you have perfect credit, but it will not be acceptable if you show a pattern of late payments. Remember, lenders are looking to see if you can manage your finances because if you can manage your finances, you will probably make your mortgage payments on time. Managing your finances means that you live within your budget, you pay your accounts on time, and you have an emergency fund to handle unexpected expenses.

- Proportion of balances to credit limits on revolving accounts is too high

  Your credit score goes down when you use more than 30 percent of your available credit. You may be making on-time payments, but if you are about to max out the credit cards, you will have a low credit score. The credit score sees high credit card balances as a high risk and assumes you could eventually find yourself in a position where you could not make your payment.

  To improve your credit score, you will need to pay down your credit card balances. The lower the balances, the better the credit score. If you had surplus income when you completed your budget in step 2, use the surplus to pay down your credit card balances. Decreasing credit card balances is probably the easiest way to improve your credit score without the use of a credit repair company.

  Most people believe on-time payments on revolving credit accounts will give them a good credit score. Your on-time payments will help your credit score, but high balances will offset a good payment history.

- Lack of recent revolving account information

  A revolving account is a credit card for which the monthly payment changes, depending on the amount you owe. As the balance on the credit card increases, the monthly payment will increase. For those of you who do not like to use revolving credit, you will have to obtain a revolving credit card whether you like it or not. Fully

30 percent of your credit score is based on how you manage revolving credit card debt. If you do not have a revolving credit card or you do not like using credit, you will not have a high credit score, especially if you have delinquent payment history on your credit report. I think it sucks, but that is the way the credit score works.

Now, you are probably wondering, "If I have bad credit, will anyone approve me for a credit card?" You probably would not get approved for an unsecured credit card that requires your signature on the credit card agreement. With poor credit, you will have to obtain a secured credit card. A secured card will require you to make a deposit with the creditor before you are granted credit. See step 4 for more detailed information on obtaining a secured credit card.

- Length of time accounts have been established

There is not much you can do to improve your credit score if this is one of your reason statements. If you have a long credit history, the length of time your accounts have been open is probably helping your score. For more than twenty years, I have reviewed credit reports, and most credit scores improve after credit accounts have been established for five years or longer. FICO high achievers have an average account age of eleven years or more. You can try becoming an authorized user on a family member's account, but you are then allowing him or her to control your credit score. If your family member has a thirty-day late payment, your credit score will go down.

The length of credit history is also determined by delinquent accounts on your credit report. A five-year-old delinquent account deleted from your credit report could cause a decrease in your credit score if the other accounts on your report have only two-year histories.

- Too many inquiries in the last twelve months

Too many inquiries are a sign that you are acquiring new debt, and too much new debt makes you a high risk. Also, you may need to explain any inquiries on your credit report during the ninety days prior to a loan application. If you are rate shopping, don't be too concerned; the credit score will take that into account and will count any rate shopping done within a fourteen-day period as a single inquiry.

If you have poor credit and you apply for a secured credit card, do not worry about the decrease in your score. The good payment history and low balance on your new secured credit card will wipe out any negative effects of the inquiry after six months of on-time payments.

- Too few accounts currently paid as agreed

If this statement is included as one of your reasons, then you are not paying your accounts on time. You will need to review your budget to see where your money is going. If, after you review your budget, you find that you do not have enough income to pay your accounts on time, then you will need to look for other sources of income to bring the accounts current. Making a payment arrangement with the creditor to pay less than the required amount will still show as a late payment on your credit report.

- Too many accounts with balances

You may be paying your accounts on time, but you have too much debt. The credit score sees you as a high risk and assumes you may not make payments on time if you lose your job or become ill. Start working on paying off some of your accounts. When you pay off an account, do not close it. Your credit limit on the account will help your credit score.

Step 4

Improving Your Credit Score

DETERMINING YOUR CREDIT SCORE

The credit score reflects how you handle your payment history, your credit usage, the length of your credit history, and inquiries for new credit as well as new accounts opened and the type of accounts on your credit report. An overview of these areas follows.

Payment history

An acceptable payment history is a major requirement for approval on a mortgage loan. Payment history makes up 35 percent of your credit score. The credit score reviews both positive and negative payment history. Positive payment history includes accounts with no late payments. Negative payment history includes credit accounts with late payments or no payments, bankruptcies, foreclosures, tax liens, judgments, and collection accounts.

The more recent the negative information, the lower the credit score. As negative information ages, it will have less impact on your credit score. One thirty-day late payment on your credit report last month will decrease your score more than a thirty-day late payment that happened three years ago. Recent late payments on credit accounts may cause a 60- to 80-point decrease in your credit score. Even mortgage lenders concentrate on your payment history for the last two years when reviewing your credit history for loan approval.

It is important that you have two or three credit accounts with no late payments or outstanding collection accounts in the previous year. On-time payments make up 35 percent

18

of your credit score and indicate to the lender that you know how to manage your financial responsibilities. If you have late payments, bring them current. You will see some improvement in your score when these accounts are brought current but no major improvement until the delinquency is more than two years old.

The reason I recommended in step 1 that you complete your budget and start an emergency fund is that a good payment history is crucial if you want to improve your credit score and obtain approval on a mortgage loan. If you do not know where your money is going, you will have difficulty making payments on time.

The mortgage lender may request monthly payment information on accounts not reported to the CRAs to establish your credit history. Rental payments are not reported on your credit report, but the mortgage lender will request a rental payment history from your landlord. A thirty-day late payment on your rent in the last twelve months may require you to wait a year before obtaining mortgage loan approval.

Credit usage

The second largest impact on your credit score is the balance on revolving credit accounts, which represents 30 percent of your score. If your credit cards are maxed out (you have used all your available credit), your credit score will be low. Lenders call this your *credit utilization rate*, which is the balance on your credit card divided by the credit card limit. For example, if you had a Visa card with a balance of $5,000 and a credit limit of $10,000, then your credit utilization rate would be 50 percent ($5,000 ÷ $10,000 = 50 percent).

Your credit utilization rate should be less than 30 percent—the lower, the better. FICO high achievers, people with the highest credit scores, have utilization rates of 10 percent or less.

Credit usage is the second most important area to work on to improve your credit score. Pay down your credit card balances so that the credit utilization rate does not exceed 30 percent. Reducing credit card balances is the quickest way to increase your credit score.

I recently reduced my balances on three credit cards that were almost maxed out and saw a 60-point increase in my credit score.

The credit score also takes into account the balances on auto, finance company, and bank loans. However, these balances have a minor to moderate impact on your credit score. Concentrate on reducing installment loan balances after you have paid down credit card balances and established an emergency fund.

Length of credit history

The length of your credit history represents 15 percent of your credit score. The longer your credit history, the better your credit score. The credit score determines the average age of your accounts by adding the total number of years for each account and then dividing that number by the number of accounts. If you open too many new accounts, each account opened will lower the average age of your credit history and decrease your credit score. For example, you have three credit cards with a total length of credit history of twenty-four years and an average age of eight years (24 years ÷ 3 = 8). When you open a new card, you now have four credit cards with a credit history of twenty-four years and an average age of six years (24 years ÷ 4 = 6).

Inquiries for new credit

New credit represents 10 percent of your credit score. As you improve your credit score, you may be tempted with new credit card offers. Do not open new accounts unless those accounts will help increase your credit score. Too many new inquiries and new credit accounts will lower your credit score. The credit score views new applications for credit and new accounts as indications that you do not have the cash to purchase the items you need. The credit score assumes that if there is a loss of income or you have overextended yourself, you will not have the money to make payments on your credit accounts. You will not decrease your credit score when you order your personal credit report.

Types of credit used

Types of credit used represents 10 percent of your credit score. The types of credit that the credit score wants to see on your credit report are revolving credit accounts, auto loans, and mortgage loans. Revolving accounts have the greatest impact on your credit score. I have reviewed credit reports for which the only credit accounts were revolving credit, and the scores were in the range of 700–750.

OBTAINING SECURED CREDIT CARDS

If lack of revolving credit is one of the reasons your score is low, you must apply for a bank or credit union revolving credit card, as 30 percent of your credit score reflects how you manage revolving credit. If you have no revolving accounts on your credit report, you will have a difficult time in obtaining a high credit score.

If you have chosen not to use revolving credit and have no delinquent or derogatory credit, you probably can qualify for an unsecured credit card where you bank. If you have delinquent or derogatory credit on your credit report, you will need to apply for a secured credit card. A secured credit card will require that you make a deposit at the bank or credit union to establish your credit limit. A $500 deposit will give you a $500 credit limit. You will not have access to the deposit until the account is closed or if the lender changes your secured credit card to unsecured because of your on-time payment history. Apply for your secured card where you bank, ask friends to recommend a credit card, or Google "credit cards for people with poor credit."

Your secured credit card is a tool to improve your credit score. Use your secured credit card to purchase items you normally purchase with cash. Set the cash aside, and use it to pay your bill when you receive the credit card statement. Your goal is to charge and then pay off the balance immediately when you receive the credit card statement. Charge something, and then pay it off. You might leave an account balance of between $5 and $10 to show that the account is active but never more. You will need to make on-time payments on the account for six months before it will affect your score.

When applying for a secured credit card, consider the following:

- Choose a secured card that offers a low deposit. The credit score makes little distinction between a $300 credit limit and a $1,000 credit limit. The credit score is more concerned with how much of your available credit you are using. Never use more than 30 percent of your credit limit. If you have a $300 credit limit, your balance should never be more than $90. The lower the balance, the better.
- The creditor must report to Experian, Equifax, and TransUnion.
- Avoid secured credit cards with high annual membership, processing, or setup fees. These fees could be $99.95 or more and are added on your first statement, which could cause your credit utilization rate to exceed 30 percent. Your credit score would then decrease, rather than improving.
- Shop for the lowest interest rate.
- Understand the guidelines the issuer will use to transfer the account from secured to unsecured.
- Depending on the amount of derogatory information on your credit report, you may need several secured cards to increase your credit score. The credit score does not differentiate between a secured and an unsecured account.

OUTSTANDING COLLECTIONS

After you have established your good payment history, you then want to look at recent collection accounts. The more recent the collection, the lower the credit score. The goal with recent collections is to see if you can settle these accounts with the creditor and have them removed from your credit report. A collection account deleted from the credit report would remove negative credit payment history and improve your credit score. Getting the collection removed will depend on whether the account is held by the original creditor or a collection agency. The original creditor probably won't remove the account from your credit report because it has your signature on an agreement in which you promised to make on-time payments if you were granted credit. A collection agency that owns the account may consider deleting it from the credit report. If the collection account is less than two years old and cannot be deleted from the credit report, then consider paying the account in full and requesting that the statement "account paid in full" be added to the account. Paying the account in full may help because the lender is also evaluating your ability to manage your finances when reviewing your loan application. The mortgage lender is trying to determine if you are the type of person who is conscientious about making your payments on time or if you are the type of person who says, "If they can find me, I will pay them." The fact that you paid the account may make the difference between loan approval and loan denial, especially if you have a minimum credit score, and your loan is manually underwritten. A manually underwritten loan does not receive automatic approval by a computerized system and requires a review by a human to determine loan approval. A manually underwritten loan may require more documentation and explanation from you before approval.

Having a good credit score is like investing in the stock market. You will see your returns in the form of money you save from lower interest rates, which will give you lower monthly payments on credit cards and installment loans. Lower deposits or no deposits may be required when you open new accounts with utility companies, phone companies, and cable television providers, and you will make lower monthly payments on auto and home insurance. My question to you is: "What will you do with the money you save?" Maybe you can invest in the stock market or in bonds and see a good return on your investment for your retirement savings account.

In the exhibits section, the flowchart titled "Credit Score" is another resource to guide you through this process.

I wish I could tell you how much your score would increase each time you added a secured credit card or paid down credit card balances or had a negative item removed from your credit report. If I could, I would have opened a business and charged you a lot more than you paid for this book. However, there is a tool that I love to use to estimate whether my credit score will decrease or increase based on any financial action I am considering. Some of the free credit score sites have credit score simulators. They are for informational purposes only, but they can guide you in how the financial decisions you make may affect your credit score. I was thinking about putting all my credit card balances on one card. I thought that would increase my score, but when I used the simulator, my score decreased by ten points. After seeing the decrease, I remembered that my balances were spread among several cards, and if I put them on one card, then my utilization rate on that card would increase. The increase in the utilization rate over 30 percent on that one card would have caused my credit score to decrease.

The credit score simulator will give you preselected scenarios to consider. Examples include what would happen if you got a new loan or credit card, if you let your payments go past due, and if you have an account go into collection. I completed the scenario about letting an account go into collection, and the simulator said my score would drop almost 100 points. The score simulator is the best help you can get to show you how to improve your score. Credit repair companies will use the same credit score scenario and charge you $50 and up. You can do it yourself for free. I have included the websites that provide credit score simulators in the resources section.

Step 5

Reviewing Your Credit Report

In this step, you will get familiar with your credit report. The more you understand how to read your credit report, the easier the credit repair process will be. I have not included a sample credit report in this book. You can search the Internet if you need additional help understanding how to read your report.

Start reviewing your Experian and TransUnion credit reports first, since they are easy to read. After reviewing those reports, you will be more comfortable reviewing your Equifax report. Under "Credit Report Basics" on the Experian website is a good overview of an Experian credit report. All your credit reports will not contain the same information, since lenders are not required to report to all three CRAs. Major revolving credit card companies may report to all three; a retail store may report to just one.

Make a copy of your credit report, and file the original. You will make all your comments on the copy. Now review each section of the report for inaccurate information. As you go through the report, make notes or circle information that you believe is inaccurate. If you are not sure, place a question mark next to the information. Make sure you start the dispute process are soon as you receive your credit report. If you wait too long, you may have to order a new credit report to dispute inaccurate accounts.

CREDIT ACCOUNT AREAS

There are four areas on your credit report that you will be reviewing for credit repair. These areas are personal identification information, public record information, inquiries, and credit account information. Included in the credit account information are accounts with good payment history as well as delinquent or derogatory accounts. These areas will appear on all three credit reports but in different locations.

Personal identification section

Your first step in credit repair is to review the information appearing in the personal identification section of your credit report. This section will contain your name, current and previous addresses, current and previous employers, current and previous telephone numbers, and the last four digits of your Social Security number. Each time you apply for credit, new information is added to your credit report. Don't worry about street misspellings or street numbers being transposed. These mistakes are usually typos made by the person inputting the data to pull the credit report. However, if you see a street you have never lived on, employment listed where you have never worked, or a city in which you have never lived, then you have inaccurate information on your credit report, and you need to dispute this information with the CRA. Inaccurate information in this area may indicate you are a victim of identity theft.

Inaccurate information may also appear on your credit report if you are named after a family member or your name is similar to that of a family member. For example, if a father gives his name to his son, then the father is "Senior," and the son is "Junior." When applying for credit, the father and son should include the "Senior" or "Junior" in their names to prevent credit reporting being applied to the wrong credit file. Twins may also have a problem if their names are similar and their Social Security numbers are the same except for the last one or two digits. Children with names similar to their parents' and who have the same address may also have a problem with inaccurate information appearing on their credit reports.

People with common names may have this problem too. Joyce Brown is a very common name, and I have to review my credit report regularly to make sure that someone else named Brown who happens to live in my zip code area does not have her information appearing on my credit report. At one time, all my credit disappeared from my Experian credit report and appeared on my husband's because we had the same first initial and last name. I will never know how my information was added to his credit report, but it was very easy to correct. Inaccurate information in the personal identification section of your credit report is the easiest information to correct. Please do not pay a credit repair company to correct this information for you. You would be just wasting your money.

Public record information

In this section, you will normally see judgments, bankruptcies, and tax liens resulting from court cases brought against you. Information appearing in this section of the credit report is a matter of court record and is not easily disputed. Once the issue is ruled on in court, it is on record even if you did not know anything about it. Also, your disagreement with the creditor that brought the lawsuit against you is not enough to dispute the public record and have it removed from your credit report. If you truly know the judgment is not against you, then dispute it directly with the attorney who brought the suit, and provide the attorney with details explaining why it is not yours. Mistakes can easily happen to persons with similar names because some court cases do not include any additional identifying information to distinguish you from the guilty party. If the judgment or lien was filed in error, make sure you provide the court with documentation. Next, dispute the information with the CRAs and provide documentation that the liens were filed in error. The CRAs will show the lien as vacated or filed in error on your credit reports. Easy fix, if you have the documentation.

Effective July 1, 2017, the three major CRAs will not include court records on credit reports if they do not include the person's name, address, and either Social Security number or date of birth. In addition to new reporting procedures, judgments and tax liens currently on your credit report that do not have this identifying information will be removed.

If the judgment is against you, then you will need to make arrangements with the attorney representing the creditor or plaintiff to resolve the issue. Judgments remain on your credit report for seven years from the date of filing. Depending on the state you live in, the creditor may be able to refile the judgment before it expires and have the judgment reported for another seven years.

If you have filed for bankruptcy under chapter 13, the bankruptcy will remain on your credit report for seven years. A chapter 7 bankruptcy remains for ten years.

When it comes to credit repair and getting approved for a mortgage loan, judgments must be resolved before mortgage lenders will approve the loan. Judgments attach to the property and would require the mortgage lender to pay the judgment if they have to foreclose on your home should you not be able to make your mortgage payments. If you are not able to resolve the lawsuit, you will probably have to wait until it is removed from the credit report before applying for a mortgage loan. However, depending on the amount of the judgment and the funds in your bank account, if you are making monthly payments on the judgment, you might be able to get approved.

If you neglected to or just could not pay your income taxes and IRS took you to court and filed a tax lien against you, the tax lien must be paid before you apply for a mortgage loan. In some situations, you can have a payment plan with the IRS and obtain mortgage loan approval, but check with your mortgage loan officer to see if you can get approved in this situation. IRS paid tax liens remain on your credit report for seven years from the date the tax lien was paid and released. Unpaid tax liens remain on your credit report for ten years from the date of filing.

Any information appearing in the public records section is extremely damaging to your credit score. If you have information in this section, be sure to discuss it with your loan officer to find out what is required of you to obtain mortgage loan approval.

Inquiries

Two types of inquiries may appear on your credit report—hard inquiries and soft inquiries. Too many hard inquiries and newly opened credit accounts resulting from hard inquiries can reduce your credit score. Soft inquiries result from preapproved credit card offers, applying for your personal credit report, and reviews of your credit report by employers or insurance companies. Soft inquiries do not affect your credit score.

This section is extremely important to review because it may show you have been a victim of identity theft. If you see creditors in this section to whom you never applied for credit, review the credit account section to see if a new account appears. If it does, immediately call the creditor to dispute the account. The phone number should appear on your credit report, so you can notify the creditor if you think you are a victim of identity theft and find out what procedures you need to follow to get the account removed from your credit report. If no phone number appears, send a certified letter to the creditor. The creditor may require you file an identity theft affidavit. A sample affidavit can be obtained from the Federal Trade Commission at www.ftc.gov/identytheft.

Credit accounts

Credit accounts are accounts that are added to your credit report when you are approved for a credit card, buy a car, or get a loan for school or any other item you needed but did not have the money to pay for. In this section, you are looking for accounts that have a thirty-, sixty-, or ninety-day late payment. You will need to determine whether or not the late payments are accurate. If payments are inaccurate, contact the creditors to get them to send corrections to the CRA. It is preferable to contact the creditor first instead of disputing the inaccuracy with the CRA. If the late payments are accurate, then you must bring the accounts current. Depending on the number of late payments on the report, you may have to make on-time payments for up to a year before an underwriter approves you for your mortgage loan. Lenders do not want to see late payments within the twelve months prior to starting the loan application process.

Revolving credit accounts, such as your Mastercard, Visa, or store credit cards, should have low balances. As mentioned earlier, your balances should not exceed 30 percent of the available credit limit. If your utilization rate is currently at 30 percent, and you still want to see improvement in your score, pay the balances down to 10 percent or less.

Collection accounts

Collection accounts are accounts on which you were not able to pay the original creditor. When the account became delinquent, the original creditor either contracted with or sold the account to a third party to collect the payment from you. These collection accounts can be resold and may appear on your credit report several times. Collection accounts can be very difficult to work with because you may not recognize the name of the collection agency as a company to which you owe money. If you got your credit report from the Annual Credit Report Request Service, the report will show the name of the original creditor. If you do not recognize the collection agency name, you can Google the collection agency to find out what kind of accounts it specializes in collecting, and that might help you determine the original creditor. You can also contact the CRA to find out who the original creditor was. Do not dispute an account with the CRA because you do not recognize the business name on the account. Only dispute with the CRA if you are sure that you know an account is not yours. If you are not sure, dispute directly with the creditor or collection agency using letter C in the exhibits section of this book.

If a collection agency purchased the debt, the name of the original creditor should be included in the account information. The key point to remember is that the collection account will be removed from the credit report seven years from the date the original account went delinquent and not the date the collection agency added the account to the credit report. Your Experian and TransUnion credit reports will show the date the collection will be removed from the credit report. Equifax will show you the date of the original delinquency; you will need to add seven years to that date to determine when the account will be removed.

If you cannot determine the date the account went delinquent and when the account will be removed from the credit report, you can contact the CRA. The phone number or e-mail address will be on your credit report, and the CRA can tell you when the account will be removed from the report. Recent collections hurt your credit score more than a collection that is five years old. Work on the most recent collections first, and try to negotiate an account deletion or pay the account in full for a positive statement.

Charge-offs

Charge-offs are credit accounts on which you stopped making payments. After six months of no payments, the creditor stops trying to collect payment on the account. When an account is a charge-off, the creditor will either turn the account over to its collection department, contract with a third party to collect, or sell the account to a collection agency. If the account is sold, the credit report will show it as having been "sold and transferred." If the account has been sold, the account should show a zero balance. Dispute the account balance if it does not. A sold revolving credit account showing a balance will increase its utilization rate to more than 100 percent and decrease your credit score.

Rental collections

Rental collections are usually added to your credit report if you move from your apartment before the end of your lease, you are evicted for nonpayment of rent, or the landlord had to make repairs to the property that were in violation of your lease. Instead of the apartment owner trying to collect from you, he or she will contract with a collection agency to collect the amount you owe. You might not have been aware you owed the landlord money until the collection appeared on your credit report if he or she did not know where to send the final bill. Contact the collection agency to see what you can work out. If you are having difficulty working with the collection agency, contact the tenants' association in your area for assistance. For a small fee, the tenants' association will have an attorney who can guide you through the process.

Medical collections

It is easy for a medical collection to appear on your credit report without you knowing it was added. You can have a perfect payment history and see your credit score drop 30 or more points with a recent medical collection. Effective September 2017, the CRAs will prohibit medical debts from being added to your credit report until after a 180-day waiting period to allow insurance payments to be applied. For more information, go to http://nationalconsumerassistanceplan.com/. If you see a medical debt on your credit report before the 180-day waiting period has expired, you can dispute the medical collection, and it will be removed from your credit report. The 180-day waiting period does not apply to collection accounts sold to third-party collection agencies. The medical collection will be added back to the credit report if payment arrangements are not made by you or your insurance provider.

If you qualify as low income and do not have the funds to pay a hospital bill, you may be eligible for charity assistance from the hospital. Contact the hospital billing office. If you receive Medicaid and the medical provider is trying to collect, contact the Medicaid office to see if the charges are correct. If you are not responsible for the payment, send documentation to the collection agency to have the account removed from your credit report. If you are responsible for the payment, contact the medical provider and negotiate for a smaller lump sum payment or monthly payments. Do not ignore the bill.

Utility collections

Utility companies will not report good payment histories to the CRAs, but if you do not pay, the companies will surely report your delinquency. Usually, a utility collection will appear if you moved without having the utilities turned off or if the utility company did not know where to send the final bill. Utility collections are difficult to remove from your account since you contracted with the company to have utilities turned on at the property. It is best that you make payment arrangements on the outstanding amount unless you know it is inaccurate.

Utility companies will change collection agencies frequently, and it is not unusual to see the collection reported two or three times by different collection agencies. If several collection agencies are trying to collect on the same account, then dispute the accounts with the CRAs. The earlier accounts will be removed, and the most recent collection account, which you are responsible for, will remain.

Mobile phone and cable provider collections

If you change mobile phone or cable providers frequently, you may see these collections on your credit report. Normally, this is because the provider did not receive your final payment. Mobile phone and cable providers contract with new collection companies frequently, which creates duplicate accounts. Duplicate accounts are easy to locate because the collection companies are required to show the original creditor. If you see the same creditor on several collection accounts and you know you had only one account with the creditor, then dispute the duplicate accounts the same way you did with the utility companies.

Student loans

Don't worry about student loans that are current. Your student loan may appear on your credit report more than once even though you are making only one payment. Each semester that you applied for a student loan, you established a new credit account. You are making one on-time payment, and the student loan company will apply the payment to each account. If you applied for student loans for six semesters, your credit report will show six lines of good payment history.

If your school loan defaults, then you must bring the loan current. See the chapter on obtaining mortgage loan approval for more details on defaulted student loans.

Step 6

Disputing Inaccurate Credit Account Information

According to a study by the Federal Trade Commission released in February 2013, "One in five consumers had an error that was corrected by a CRA after it was disputed on at least one of their three credit reports." The Fair Credit Reporting Act (FCRA) states that inaccurate accounts must be removed from or corrected in your credit files.

When you dispute inaccurate information with a CRA, the CRA will contact the creditor or collection agency to determine if the information listed on your credit report is inaccurate. If the creditor or collection agency agrees with your dispute, then it will report this information to the CRA, and the CRA will update or remove the inaccurate information. The creditor or collection agency must respond within thirty days, or the CRA will remove the account from your credit report. If the creditor or collection agency disagrees with your dispute, then the CRA will show account as disputed, along with the date the dispute was initiated.

The CRA will give you the opportunity to provide a one-hundred-word statement, in which you can explain why the information is inaccurate. Do not include a statement on your credit report. If you do place a statement on your credit report, be sure to have it removed when it is no longer relevant. I have seen five-year-old statements referencing delinquent credit that no longer appeared on the credit report. During the loan application process, you will have an opportunity to provide a written statement and documentation stating why the information is inaccurate.

Inaccurate information is not the same as a dispute with the creditor or collection agency about whether or not you paid for the services rendered or the amount you owe. Inaccurate information is information that was reported incorrectly, for which you have proof of the inaccuracy. If you do not have proof, it may be difficult to get the disputed account removed or corrected on the credit report. If the disputed account is affecting your ability to get approved for a mortgage loan, you may have to bite the bullet and pay the outstanding balance so your mortgage can get approved. The benefits of home ownership will far outweigh your belief that the creditor is wrong, and you are right.

INACCURATE INFORMATION YOU SHOULD DISPUTE

1. Inaccurate current or previous addresses reported in the personal identification section (e.g., Your credit report lists an address in New York City, and you have lived in Texas all your life.)
2. Inaccurate current or previous employers reported in the personal identification section
3. Outstanding collection accounts that are out of date and should have been removed from the credit report seven years after the date of original delinquency
4. Duplicate reporting of collection accounts
5. Late payments for which you have documentation showing that the payments were made on time
6. Accounts that you did not open
7. Incorrect account balances
8. Accounts not showing "included in bankruptcy"
9. Accounts with incomplete information

It is extremely important that you dispute with the CRA only those accounts you know are inaccurate, and if needed, you have the documentation to support your claim. If you are not sure, dispute the debt directly with the original creditor or collection agency. The Fair Credit

Reporting Act allows you to dispute with the company that furnished the information to the CRA.

A disputed account is not included in the credit score calculation, which is the reason most lenders will not approve a credit file with disputed accounts. A disputed account does not provide an accurate picture of your credit risk, and the mortgage lenders may require you to contact the CRA or creditor to have the dispute removed from the credit report before processing your loan application.

Removing a disputed account from your credit report will probably require you to contact the company that reported the delinquency. You can try contacting the CRA and saying that you no longer dispute the account; however, some CRAs require the original creditor or collection agency to report that the account is no longer in dispute before removing "account in dispute status" from the credit report. If the disputed account has an outstanding balance, you will probably have to negotiate the payment before the creditor removes the dispute status from the account. Paying the balance is not a bad thing unless you do not have the money.

If you are not sure a credit or collection agency account is yours or you do not recognize the creditor or collection agency, always send a letter of dispute directly to the company reporting the information on your credit report.

Using a credit repair company that is not familiar with what is required to obtain mortgage approval can hurt your chances of getting approved. Some credit repair companies will dispute all the information on your credit report whether it's accurate or not to see what negative information will be removed from the report. The problem with this is that the furnishers have thirty days to respond to the CRA. If they do not respond within the thirty days, the CRA will delete the accounts from your credit report, even if the information is accurate. If the furnishers report on a later date that the account information is accurate, the delinquent accounts will return to your credit report. Lenders pull a credit report at loan application and another one before loan closing. Unfortunately, if these delinquent accounts reappear before the lender pulls the final credit report, they can negatively affect your credit score, and your mortgage loan application may be denied. How heartbreaking for you and how embarrassing it would be to notify family and friends, your current landlord, and the moving company that you would not be getting your new home.

OUT-OF-DATE REPORTING

The Fair Credit Reporting Act, as amended in 1997, requires creditors to report the date of first delinquency to the national CRAs. The act was amended to make sure everyone was on the same page when it came time to delete an account from a credit report.

Out-of-date reporting is one area in which credit repair companies make you believe they have helped you clean up your credit. You can do this yourself. It probably won't take more than an hour to review the credit accounts to see that one account listed is one you had in college ten years ago. You are the best person to determine if the delinquent account is more than seven years old. Out-of-date reporting usually occurs when the original creditor sells the account to a collection agency, and the collection agency sells the account to another collection agency. The new collection agency may report inaccurate information because they did not receive the correct information when they purchased the account. Here is an example of the credit history of a delinquent account:

Jazzy Clothing Store
Date of First Delinquency 3/1/2012
Account Charged Off 9/2012
Sold to Sunburst Collection Agency
Account Status: Sold or transferred
Balance shows zero.

Sunburst Collection Co.

Now owns debt, reports delinquent 3/2012

Cannot collect and sells to XYZ Collection Agency

Account Status: Sold or transferred

XYZ Collection Agency

Now owns debt, reports delinquent 3/1/2012

Debtor pays debt on 4/1/2017

Account Status: Paid collection 4/2017

CRA deletes all three accounts 3/1/2019

The collection accounts and the original delinquent account remain on your credit report for seven years from the date of original delinquency. The original account became delinquent in March 2012, so all accounts will be removed in March 2019.

The Fair Credit Reporting Act limits the amount of time that delinquent and derogatory information can remain on your credit report:

- 2 years—credit inquiries
- 7 years—late payments, charge-offs, collections, paid tax liens, foreclosures, judgments, chapter 13 bankruptcies, dismissed chapter 7 bankruptcies
- 10 years—chapter 7 bankruptcies, unpaid tax liens

Good payment histories can remain on the credit report indefinitely.

The statute of limitations on an item remaining on the credit report should not be confused with your responsibility to repay the creditor if an account becomes a charge-off or collection. Removing an account from your credit report does not mean you no longer owe on the account. The Fair Credit Reporting Act says the delinquent account can no longer affect your credit rating after the number of years specified above. You still are obligated to pay the account, and each state has a statute of limitations on the length of time a creditor is given to take you to court to seek payment. You can go to http://www.bankrate.com/finance/credit-cards/state-statutes-of-limitations-for-old-debts-1.aspx and locate the statute of limitations for your state. In the state of Texas, the creditor cannot take you to court after four years from the date of your last payment. After seven years, the delinquent credit is removed from your credit report. The delinquent or derogatory accounts may not be able to hurt you on your credit report, but you will still be liable for the debt, and the creditor or collection agency can continue to call you to collect.

Dispute Process Summary

When reviewing your credit report in step 5, you were provided with an overview of many of the accounts that you would see on your credit report and suggestions on how to resolve the delinquency. In this step, you were provided with examples of inaccurate information you should dispute on your credit report and information on how long delinquent accounts can remain on your credit report. The information you have read should have prepared you to know what you can dispute on your credit report.

Below is a summary of the dispute process that you can use along with the flowcharts for credit repair and handling outstanding collections and delinquencies.

- First, you will want to review your credit report for inaccurate information. Before you go directly to the delinquent credit account section, take a few minutes to read through your credit report. Pay attention to where the sections are located on each credit report because Experian, TransUnion, and Equifax will not use the same section format on the credit report. Also, your Equifax credit report has an excellent credit summary to help you understand your credit score. Be sure to locate Experian's report number, TransUnion's file number, and Equifax's confirmation number on the report because you will need these numbers when you file a dispute.

- If you are disputing by mail, locate the mailing address you are required to use when you return your dispute letter. The address is usually listed at the end of the report.

- Review one credit report at a time. You can use the dispute form returned with your credit report, the Credit Bureau Dispute Form included in the exhibits section at the end of this book, or you can dispute on-line. In step 5, you were provided information to determine what you are disputing.

- Begin by disputing inaccurate information in the personal identification section, and the inquiries section. These sections are the easiest to dispute and may help you discover if you are a victim of identity theft. In the inquiries section, you are disputing inquires where you never applied for credit. The inquiry section is titled differently on each credit report. On your Experian credit report, this will show as "Inquiries Shared with Others," on TransUnion credit report, this will show as "Regular Inquiries," and on Equifax credit report, it will show as "Inquiries that may impact your credit rating/score."

- Next, review the information in the public records section. Information included in this section cannot be disputed with the CRA unless you have court documentation showing the credit report information is inaccurate. If you have delinquent information in this section, contact the company or agency filing the judgment against you or the court where the judgment was filed. You will have to work out a settlement with them.

- Now you will begin disputing inaccurate delinquencies on your credit report. Use the Credit Bureau Dispute Form included in the exhibits section and check the reason you are disputing the account. You will enter the reason for the dispute for each credit account. Once you have disputed each inaccurate account, mail the form to the CRA using the mailing address on your credit report. You can also use the form provided by the CRA or dispute online. Be sure you include your report, file, or confirmation number on any documents mailed to the CRA.

- If you are not sure if the delinquent account is yours, then mail letter C to the original creditor or collection agency to prevent a dispute statement from being added to the credit account. Credit accounts that show disputed on your credit report can affect your ability to get approved for your mortgage loan.

- Within 30 days, the CRA will send you an email or letter stating if the account has been deleted or updated. If the account has been deleted or updated with a positive statement, there is nothing more you need to provide to the CRA. You have been successful in providing an accurate picture of your credit history to lenders.

- If you still need to improve your credit score, review your credit score reason statements to see what steps you can take to improve your score. Make sure your credit utilization rate is less than 30 percent since most credit scores can be improved by simply paying down the balance on credit cards. Review steps 3 and 4.

- If you have accurate delinquent accounts remaining on your credit report, and you need to improve your credit score to get approved on the mortgage loan, your next step is to work toward a settlement with the creditor or collection agency to delete the account from your credit report or to add a positive statement. You will want to work first on delinquencies that have occurred in the previous two years prior to your loan application date. Review step 7.

- If you receive collections letters in the mail, do not ignore them. You will have 30 days to respond to the collection agency to determine if the account is accurate. Mail the letter C to collection agency by certified mail. The agency will respond to you in 30 days. When you receive the response letter, please review for accuracy. Information may be included in the response that you can use to delete inaccurate information from your credit report.

- After you have completed this process and you still do not have the desired credit score to apply for a mortgage loan, then you will need to work on making on-time payments on two or three credit cards or other installment accounts until your credit score improves. You can also wait until the negative information becomes out-of-date and is removed from your credit report. Most negative information will be deleted from the credit report seven years from the date of original delinquency.

- If you still need help, contact a HUD approved housing counseling agency or a mortgage loan officer. A housing counselor can help you with your budget and help you understand how to read your credit report. A mortgage loan officer can advise you what you must correct on your credit report to be approved on a mortgage loan, and if necessary, refer you to a reputable credit repair company.

Step 7

In this step, we will discuss how to handle delinquent and outstanding collection accounts. You should not begin this step until you have completed steps 1, 2, and 6. In this step, we assume the following:

1. You have reviewed a recent copy of your credit report, credit score, and reason statements.

2. You have completed your budget, and you know how much surplus income you have available to settle a delinquent or collection account.

3. You have already disputed any inaccurate information on your credit report with Experian, Equifax, and TransUnion.

If you have not completed the above steps, go back and finish those steps and then return to this one.

The key to determining if you should pay, settle, or ignore a delinquent or collection account will depend on how the account affects your credit score and your ability to get approved for a mortgage loan. If your reason statements included "Number of accounts with delinquency" or "Time since most recent delinquency is too short," you will have to decide how to handle the delinquent accounts. You must decide if you are going to pay the account in full, settle the account with the creditor or collection agency, or ignore the account because it does not affect your ability to get approved for your mortgage loan.

In this step, you must have surplus income to pay or settle the delinquent accounts and outstanding collections not removed from your credit report in step 6. If you do not have the extra money, continue working on rebuilding your credit by making on-time payments on current accounts. Work on trying to save money so later in the credit repair process you can negotiate settlements.

DISPUTE WITH THE ORIGINAL CREDITOR OR COLLECTION AGENCY

In step 6, you reviewed your credit accounts and disputed inaccurate information with the CRAs. At this point, the inaccurate information should have been removed from or updated on your credit report. Now you will dispute with the original creditor or the collection agency to see if you can have the negative account removed from your credit report or get some additional information about it.

When you dispute with a creditor or collection agency, complete letter C and send the dispute letter by certified mail. Certified mail allows you to track when the creditor or collection agency receives your letter. The Fair Credit Reporting Act requires the creditor or collection agency to respond to your request within thirty days. If the creditor does not respond within thirty days, you can provide the CRA with a copy of your letter and the certified mail receipt from www.usps.gov. With this information, the CRA may remove the account from your credit report.

The creditor or collection agency can respond to your dispute letter showing the name of the original creditor, the date of delinquency, and the amount owed. I have seen responses showing delinquency dates more than seven years prior, which means the account should not be on the credit report. You can submit a copy of your letter to the CRA for removal in such a case.

However, there is a good chance that the creditor or collection agency will provide you with proof that the account is yours. If the account is yours, you will need to make arrangements to pay it either in full or in a settlement.

After you have disputed all the inaccurate information on your credit report and received confirmation that the remaining accounts belong to you, then you need to decide how you will handle the delinquent or derogatory information still on your credit report. You have three choices:

1. Pay the account in full.
2. Negotiate a settlement with the creditor or collection agency.
3. Ignore the account if it does not affect your approval for the mortgage loan.

PAY THE ACCOUNT IN FULL

When would you pay the account in full?

1. You know that the account is yours.
2. You have the funds to pay the account in full.
3. The creditor refuses to negotiate a settlement.
4. The delinquent or derogatory account will affect your loan approval.

If you know that the account is yours, the best thing to do is pay the account, especially if it is within two years of your loan application. The FHA's *TOTAL Mortgage Scorecard User Guide* states, "Refer recommendation requires the borrower to provide an explanation for major indications of derogatory credit, such as judgments and collections, and any minor indications within the past two years." Your application will say a lot about your ability to manage your finances if you have paid the account yourself rather than waiting for the underwriter to require you to pay it, especially if you have a borderline credit score and your loan is manually underwritten rather than being approved through an automated underwriting system. If you do not have the funds to make the full payment, wait until you have saved the full amount, and then approach the creditor or collection agency to pay in full or make a settlement on the account. Do not make payment arrangements. If you set up a payment arrangement and have a setback and cannot make the payment, you have created a new recent delinquency, which will decrease your credit score.

Some credit repair companies will continue to dispute an account, hoping that they might get lucky, and the CRA will remove the account from your credit report. I have seen credit repair companies continue to dispute accurate delinquent and derogatory accounts even when their clients admit these were their accounts, and they did not make the payments. Continuing to dispute is a waste of time, and the credit repair company is charging you for this when they know the creditor or collection agency will not delete the account. If you have the funds to pay a delinquent account, pay it and move on. While you or the credit repair company continue to dispute the account, hoping it will be deleted from your credit report, you may miss out on funds from down payment assistance programs, low interest rates, or your dream home. The money you are paying the credit repair company could be used to obtain secured credit cards to improve your payment history or to negotiate a settlement on outstanding collections, which can increase your credit score.

NEGOTIATE A SETTLEMENT WITH THE CREDITOR OR COLLECTION AGENCY

Usually, an account that has been charged or written off will have a much larger balance than the amount you originally owed. The increased amount is due to late payment fees and penalties. It is not unusual for an account with a credit limit of $300 to have a balance of $1,800 after four or five years.

You may have a difficult time negotiating a settlement for a lower amount with original creditors who do not sell their accounts to third parties to collect. Since original creditors have your signature on the credit agreement and documentation showing your payment history, they may request full payment. Collections agencies that purchase debts from the original creditors may be more agreeable to negotiating a settlement for a lower amount.

When negotiating a settlement, follow the order below:

1. Negotiate for a lesser payoff amount.
2. Negotiate for the account to be removed from the credit report.
3. Negotiate for a letter of release.

Don't ask for all three of these at once. If you ask for all three at the same time, the collector may not believe you are serious about settling the account. If you cannot come to an agreement on any of these items, just hang up. You can always call back at a later date and get a collector who might be more agreeable to working out a settlement on your terms.

When negotiating a settlement, make sure the creditor or collection agency provides you information in writing detailing how it will report your payment history to the CRA. If the creditor or collection agency reports "settled for less than the full amount," then you have created a more recent delinquency on your credit report and will probably see a decrease in your credit score.

You probably will not get every creditor and collection agency reporting on your credit report to delete its account. If the one you are talking with will not delete, just hang up and call the next one on your list. If you have six negative accounts, you may only need to get two deleted to improve your score enough to qualify for a mortgage loan. Your goal is to get as many deletions as you can.

My good friend Chris Ebert, a paralegal with a law firm in Dallas, Texas, has been doing credit repair and debt settlement since 2003. He taught credit repair classes with me at Dallas County for six years and created a collector's script and a debt settlement script to use when working with collection agencies. These scripts are excellent and will help keep you on track when talking to collection agencies. The debt settlement script is included in the exhibits section. You can also go to https://xcreditrepair.com/xcr_signup/ for videos explaining how to use the scripts and printable copies of the scripts. The website also includes a credit repair course as a free video. The website goes into more detail on how to work with collection agencies than I have provided in this book.

IGNORE THE ACCOUNT

Three things will determine whether you should ignore an account.

1. Ignore the account if it does not have a negative impact on your mortgage loan approval.
2. Ignore the account if paying the account will not increase credit score.
3. Ignore the account if it is almost seven years old and will soon fall off the credit report.

An account that is more than five years old will probably have little impact on your credit score unless you don't have any accounts showing good payment history.

If you decide to ignore a collection account, remember the collection agency can sell the account to a new collection agency, and the new agency will create a new recent delinquent account on your credit report, which will decrease your credit score. You may see this as not fair, but remember, on your original credit agreement, you gave your promise to pay the creditor. That promise is not canceled out because you lost the income to make payments on the account or you decided not to pay because you had a dispute with the creditor. You are still responsible for payment.

I developed a credit repair flowchart to assist you in handling outstanding collection accounts. You can find the chart in the exhibits section at the end of this book.

When changes occur to your credit report, you will receive e-mail alerts from the websites from which you obtained your free credit scores. These alerts will let you know if your score has increased or decreased, if new inquiries have been added to your credit report, and if there are other changes you need to know about. If you want to monitor your credit report and score more frequently, register with a credit monitoring service. By monitoring the free credit score websites or purchasing a credit monitoring service, you will know when your credit score is high enough to qualify you for your mortgage loan.

Mortgage lenders review four areas to determine if you qualify for a mortgage loan: your credit score, your income stability, whether you have sufficient income to support the mortgage payment, and the funds you have available to pay the down payment and closing costs. If your credit score is low, the other qualifying items will not be considered. You can have perfect rental payment history, but if you are consistently late in paying credit accounts, you are considered a poor credit risk. You need a good credit score before the lender will review your qualifications for a mortgage loan.

CREDIT SCORE

Of course, the higher the credit score, the better. A high score indicates to the lender that there is minimal risk that you will default on your mortgage payments. A low credit score indicates a high risk and tells the lender that you cannot be counted on you to make your mortgage payments on time.

Both the credit score and mortgage lender review credit reports for good payment history and minimal debt. Good payment history and minimal debt represent 65 percent of your credit score. If you do not have good payment history on your credit report, you must start at this point first. Paying off outstanding collections on your credit report will not show good payment history. You can pay off all the outstanding collections on your credit report and still not see an increase in your credit score. Lenders want to see that you can manage your credit obligations and not just pay off delinquent accounts when you are trying to obtain mortgage loan approval.

If you have the minimum credit score required by the lender and your credit score does not show good payment history on three credit accounts, you may be required to show good payment history on alternative credit. Examples of alternative credit are payment on utilities, life insurance, or other accounts that you pay on time but that do not report to the CRAs.

INCOME STABILITY

You must have a source of income to qualify for a mortgage loan. The income can be from your job, self-employment, Social Security, and/or a pension. If you receive child support, you can decide if you want to use child support income to qualify for the mortgage loan. You will be required to provide documentation to support that you receive the income. If you are self-employed, the lender will use your net profit from IRS Form 1040, Schedule C to determine income stability.

SUFFICIENT INCOME TO SUPPORT THE MORTGAGE PAYMENT

The lender will review your income and debt to estimate the sales price of the home you can purchase. Make sure you speak with a loan officer to determine your home purchase price, especially if you have a taste for champagne and a pocketbook for a beer.

FUNDS FOR DOWN PAYMENT AND CLOSING COSTS

You should have at least 3–5 percent of the sales price saved for your down payment. Depending on whether there are a few homes for sale, which is considered a seller's market, or a lot of homes for sale, which is considered a buyer's market, and the location and condition of the house you are purchasing, these conditions will determine if you will need additional funds for closing costs. In a buyer's market, the seller will usually pay for repairs and closing costs. In a seller's market, they usually will not pay any additional costs. On an FHA loan, which accepts minimum credit scores, the down payment is 3.5 percent of the purchase price and must come from your savings. The down payment funds cannot be borrowed.

A LENDER'S VIEW OF DELINQUENT AND DEROGATORY ACCOUNTS

A mortgage lender hires an underwriter to review your application to determine if you will repay the mortgage loan promptly. Payment history is an extremely important part of the approval process. The FHA's *Single-Family Housing Policy Handbook* (HUD Handbook 4000.1) provides the following guidelines to assist the underwriter in determining loan approval:

The underwriter must evaluate the Borrower's payment histories in the following order: (1) previous housing expenses and related expenses, including utilities; (2) installment debts; and (3) revolving accounts.

(1) Satisfactory Credit

The underwriter may consider a Borrower to have an acceptable payment history if the Borrower has made all housing and installment debt payments on time for the previous 12 months and has no more than two 30-day late Mortgage Payments or installment payments in the previous 24 months.

The underwriter may approve the Borrower with an acceptable payment history if the Borrower has no major derogatory credit on revolving accounts in the previous 12 months.

Major derogatory credit on revolving accounts must include any payments made more than 90 Days after the due date, or three or more payments more than 60 Days after the due date.

(2) Payment History Requiring Additional Analysis

If a Borrower's credit history does not reflect satisfactory credit as stated above, the Borrower's payment history requires additional analysis.

The Mortgagee must analyze the Borrower's delinquent accounts to determine whether late payments were based on a disregard for financial obligations, an inability to manage debt, or extenuating circumstances. The Mortgagee must document this analysis in the mortgage file. Any explanation or documentation of delinquent accounts must be consistent with other information in the file.

Guidelines for underwriting other loan products, such as conventional loans, will be similar to the FHA's requirement to determine if you have the ability and the intent to pay your bills on time before granting loan approval. If you want to read the full credit underwriting guidelines for the FHA, refer to the web address in the resources section.

Delinquent and outstanding collections on your credit report are major considerations in your loan approval. The underwriter may approve your loan if you provide documentation that the delinquency was related to extenuating circumstances. Extenuating circumstances include loss of income, illness, and any other situation that was beyond your control. Also, lenders will not approve borrowers who have had a foreclosure, a deed in lieu of foreclosure, a short sale, or a chapter 7 bankruptcy within three years of the loan application. After one year of good payment history in a chapter 13 bankruptcy and permission from the bankruptcy trustee, you can apply for a mortgage loan. Judgments and IRS tax liens must be paid and released. The FHA gives mortgage lenders the ability to make their individual guidelines stricter than those of the FHA. Your mortgage lender will advise you if its loan products have longer waiting periods.

School loans must be current to obtain a mortgage loan approval. Defaulted school loans are just like other delinquent accounts on a credit report and will remain on your credit report for seven years before they are removed. However, school loans never go away, especially if you are applying for an FHA mortgage loan. The lender will order a property appraisal and also request a Credit Alert Interactive Voice Response System (CAIVRS) report on your Social Security number and date of birth in the federal computer system. Your school loan may not show on your credit report, but it will show up in the CAIVRS system as a default. If you have a defaulted student loan, contact your student loan agency to make payment arrangements. One year of good payment history is required for mortgage loan approval.

The CAIVRS is used to determine if you have defaulted on any other government loans. Any outstanding government loan must be in good standing to get approved for a government loan. If you have a minimum credit score, you will want to apply for an FHA loan because the qualifying credit score is lower than for other loan products.

CONTACT A MORTGAGE LENDER

Once you have your minimum mortgage lender credit score from myfico.com, contact a mortgage lender to determine if you meet the other qualifications for mortgage approval. When you contact a lender, you will speak with a loan officer. The loan officer or originator is knowledgeable about the requirements for loan approval and can help you through the process. He or she can advise you concerning your credit qualifications and interest rates and recommend loan products.

The more you have done to prepare yourself for the mortgage process, the easier the loan process and the faster the approval.

While you are working hard to improve your credit score, there are a few things you need to be aware of that can affect your loan approval. Please pay close attention to all the items listed below. If any of the below apply to you and you are not certain how to handle the situation, please contact a mortgage loan officer to answer your questions.

PAY ON TIME

Pay before the credit statement due date. Pay your credit statement immediately upon receipt. The easiest way to see a credit score decrease is to have one thirty-day late payment.

PAY INSTALLMENT LOANS ON TIME

Installment loans include auto loans, bank or credit union loans, and finance company loans. You should have no late payments for twelve months before applying for a mortgage loan.

PAY RENT ON TIME

Just like your other accounts, rent must be paid on time. If you cannot make on-time payments where you currently live, the mortgage lender will doubt if you can make on-time payments on your mortgage loan. No thirty-day late payments on your rent if you are serious about getting your mortgage loan approved.

AVOID NEW DEBT

New debt affects your credit score and could lower the purchase price of the home you qualify to buy. If you must incur new debt, contact your mortgage loan officer to see how the new debt will affect your loan approval. If you have made a loan application, remember even if you are preapproved, you have not received final loan approval. Your credit report will be pulled a second time just before closing. Wait until after loan closing and funding to purchase new items for your home.

DO NOT COSIGN

You may think that you are helping a family member or a friend, but you are taking on new debt that can affect your ability to qualify for a mortgage loan. A cosigner assumes full liability for the loan if the borrower does not pay, plus any late fees or collection costs. If the person you are trying to help is late in making a payment, the late payment will appear on your credit report. The lender can also place a judgment against you and the person you were trying to help if he or she defaults on the loan. If you want to help, give your family member or friend the money to make a larger down payment. The best thing to do is just say no.

LOCATE YOUR DIVORCE DECREE BEFORE APPLYING FOR YOUR LOAN

Even if you were married and divorced twenty years ago, the lender will still require a copy of your divorce decree. If you live in a community property state like Texas, the mortgage lender is concerned about any community property that is still in your name.

PAY SCHOOL LOANS

Unpaid school loans never go away. If you know that your school loan will become due and you have not heard from the lender, contact the lender immediately. You do not want your school loans to go into a delinquent status. A delinquent status could delay your loan approval for twelve months or longer.

COMMUNITY PROPERTY STATES

In community property states, the underwriter will consider all debt of both spouses even if you are the only one applying for the loan. Review your spouse's credit report before you make a loan application. If the nonqualifying spouse has debt, the amount of home loan you qualify for may decrease.

COURT-ORDERED CHILD SUPPORT PAYMENTS

If you neglected to make child support payments, you might not receive mortgage loan approval. If you are behind in child support payments, contact the office accepting your payments to see what can be done to bring them current.

AUTO REPOSSESSIONS

Whether voluntary or involuntary, both the credit score and the mortgage lender look at a repossession as derogatory credit. Review all your options before you return your auto to the dealer. You may have completed all your paperwork at the dealership, but the auto dealer and the financing company are two separate companies. Try to see if you can sell the auto or work out payment arrangements with the company providing the financing.

When you return your car to the dealer, you may still owe a balance on the loan. If the dealer can resell your auto, the proceeds will go toward the balance on your loan and reduce the amount you owe to the financing company.

DISAGREEMENT WITH A CREDITOR

Don't stop payments because of a disagreement with a creditor. The creditor will charge-off the debt, and you may still have to pay the debt in full to get approved for a mortgage loan.

AVOID BANKRUPTCY

Make this your last option. If there is one sign that says you have trouble managing your finances, bankruptcy is that sign. Mortgage lenders consider you a higher risk when you have filed bankruptcy. If you are receiving too many collection calls and you do not have the money to pay, then send the collector a letter asking them to stop calling you. The Fair Debt Practices Collection Act (FDPCA) requires the collector to stop calling you when they receive a cease communications letter. Use letter C in the "Exhibits" section to stop collection agencies from contacting you. Send the letter to the collection agency by certified mail.

If you have filed bankruptcy

If you have filed bankruptcy, review schedule A of your bankruptcy petition, which lists all the credit accounts included in the bankruptcy filing. Review the delinquent credit accounts on your credit report and make sure those accounts show "included in bankruptcy." If the accounts do not indicate they were included in the bankruptcy, send a copy of the schedule to the CRAs and request that they update your credit report.

DO NOT CLOSE ACCOUNTS

You may want to close out accounts that you no longer are using. If you close out a revolving credit card account, the credit limit is not used in determining your utilization rate. A closed account could lower your credit score because it may increase your utilization rate greater than 30 percent. Close unwanted accounts after loan closing and funding.

AVOID NEW DELINQUENCIES FROM OLD COLLECTIONS OR CHARGE-OFFS

Dispute new collection letters with letter C. Unless these accounts are settled or paid, they can be sold or transferred to new collection agencies, creating a new delinquent account, which will lower your credit score.

MAKE PAYMENT ARRANGEMENTS

Make arrangements to pay for any new medical services if you can't pay in full to prevent new delinquencies on your credit report.

ASK A FAMILY MEMBER TO ADD YOU TO A REVOLVING CREDIT ACCOUNT

Ask if you can be added as an authorized user on a family member's revolving credit account. Make sure that the primary cardholder makes timely payments, the utilization rate is less than 30 percent, and the account has a long credit history. If the account does not meet these criteria, your credit score might decrease instead of increasing.

ATTEND A HOMEBUYER EDUCATION CLASS

A homebuyer education class will help you decide if you are ready for homeownership.

Everyone is looking for a quick fix when it comes to credit repair. You may be too over-whelmed and frightened to try to do the credit repair yourself. With so many credit repair companies advertising how easily they can repair your credit, you will probably feel like the best way to repair your credit is to pay someone to do it for you.

When most people hear the term "credit repair," they immediately assume that it is something they cannot do themselves. However, those advertisements can be misleading. The client in the advertisement had the court judgment deleted because it was out of date, or the court judgment belonged to someone else with a similar name and should not have been on the credit report in the first place. You enter into an agreement with the credit repair company thinking your judgment can be removed your credit report, but it can't if the judgment is valid.

I can understand why people would believe they cannot repair their credit themselves. I know the feeling. It is hard to achieve your goal if you do not believe you can achieve it. I wanted to lose weight and just knew I could not do it myself without the magic pill, the exercise equipment, the exercise videos, and whatever else was on the market that was promising me I could lose all the weight I wanted in two weeks. It took a long time for me to realize that I needed to make the commitment to lose weight. However, after I made the commitment to eating healthy, watching my food portions, and exercising, the weight came off. Not as fast as I would have liked, but it came off and is still coming off. Credit repair is the same. You must make the commitment to do the credit repair yourself.

I hope this book has given you the information and the confidence to know that you can repair your credit yourself. I know you can because I taught a credit repair class for fourteen years and met many people who were able to improve their credit and get approved for mortgage loans without the help of a credit repair company.

Credit Repair for Mortgage Loan Approval, unlike other credit repair books on the market, is specifically designed to help you improve your credit so that you can get approved for a mortgage loan. Things may not happen as quickly as you would like, but you will get the most benefit if you do it yourself. You will also have the pride of knowing that you did it yourself, and you will have the skills to maintain good credit for the rest of your life.

Get rid of your fear, take the first step, and before you know it, your credit score will be high enough to get approved for a mortgage loan and achieve the dream of homeownership. I wish you the best on your journey!

Remember, you handle the easy stuff, and let credit repair companies handle the hard stuff.

Resources

CREDIT REPORTING AGENCIES (CRAS)

All three CRAs have credit learning/education pages on their websites, which discuss topics like credit report basics, managing credit scores, and identity theft, and they provide a glossary of credit-related terms.

Experian.com—click on Education.

TransUnion.com—click on Credit Education.

Equifax.com—click on Learn & Support.

The National Consumer Assistance Plan provides changes to how information is reported by Equifax, Experian, and TransUnion. See http://www.nationalconsumerassistanceplan.com/about/.

FREE CREDIT REPORTS AND CREDIT SCORES

- **Bankrate.com**—Free credit report from TransUnion using VantageScore 3. The TransUnion credit report provides information to help you increase your credit score. The timeline feature included with the credit report advises if closing an account will lower your credit score.
- **CreditKarma.com**—Free VantageScore 3 with Equifax and TransUnion credit reports.
- **CreditSesame.com**—Free VantageScore 3 and TransUnion credit report.
- **Credit.com**—Free FICO 8 credit score from Experian.
- **Quizzle.com**—Free VantageScore 3 with TransUnion credit report.
- **AnnualCreditReport.com**—Free credit report every twelve months from Experian, Equifax, and TransUnion. Will not include credit scores.
- **Experian.com**—Free credit report and FICO 8 score every thirty days with Experian. Excellent summary of credit report and credit score showing your credit utilization rate.

IDENTITY THEFT

- **Identitytheft.gov**—Step-by-step instructions on how to report identity theft and get a recovery plan.
- **CreditSesame.com**—In the Identity Restoration section, free restoration documents are available for download.

CREDIT SCORES

- **FICO**—Formerly the Fair Isaac Corporation, it is the developer of the FICO credit score. *Understanding Credit Scores* is an excellent booklet providing detailed information on the credit score developed by FICO. It's available for download at http://www.myfico.com/Downloads/Files/myFICO_UYFS_Booklet.pdf.
  Purchase your credit report at myfico.com, and use the FICO score simulator at https://www.myfico.com/FICOCreditScoreEstimator/Estimator.aspx? for suggestions on how to increase your score.
- **Reasoncode.org**—Powered by VantageScore 3, this is an excellent resource to help you understand the reason statements included with your credit score. See https://www.reasoncode.org/.
- **Speakingofcredit.com**—Barry Paperno, with more than forty years of experience in the credit industry, answers questions on how to increase your credit score. Mr. Paperno helped me understand credit scoring when I began teaching my credit repair class. Go to https://speakingofcredit.com/.

CREDIT REPAIR

- **Xpert Credit Repair**—Free credit repair course available at https://xcreditrepair. com/xcr_signup/. On this website, you can print.pdf copies of the credit bureau dispute form, letter C with instructions on how to use the form, and the debt settlement script form which are included in the exhibits section.

- **Federal Trade Commission**—FTC.com is the website of the Federal Trade Commission, which is responsible for the Fair Credit Reporting Act (FCRA), Fair and Accurate Credit Reporting Act (FACT), and Fair Debt Practices Collection Act (FDPCA). To file a complaint or have questions answered, call 1-877-FTC-HELP or 1-877-382-4357. The FTC will not act as your attorney.

  Excellent article concerning your rights when dealing with debt collectors under the FDPCA at https://www.consumer.ftc.gov/articles/0149-debt-collection.

  A copy of the Credit Repair Organizations Act is available at https://www.ftc.gov/ enforcement/statutes/credit-repair-organizations-act.

  "Credit Repair: How to Help Yourself"—See article at https://www.consumer.ftc. gov/articles/0058-credit-repair-how-help-yourself#croa.

CREDIT EDUCATION

- **Experian.com**—Extensive glossary of credit-related terms: http://www.experian. com/blogs/ask-experian/credit-education/faqs/glossary/.

  Understanding your Experian credit report: http://www.experian.com/blogs/ask-experian/credit-education/report-basics/understanding-your-experian-credit-report/.

- **Consumer Finance Protection Bureau**—Excellent federal website that answers hundreds of financial questions to help you make more informed choices about your money. See https://www.consumerfinance.gov/ask-cfpb/. Also provides a list of federal laws designed to protect consumers: https://www.consumerfinance.gov/learnmore/.

- **The Department of Housing and Urban Development (HUD)**—To find a HUD housing counselor, see https://www.hudexchange.info/housing-and-homeless-assistance/, or call 1-800-569-4287.

- **The Federal Housing Administration (FHA)**—Credit underwriting guidelines for automated and manual loan underwriting are located on pages 177–322 of the FHA guidelines for approving mortgage loans: https://portal.hud.gov/hudportal/documents/huddoc?id=40001HSGH.pdf.

- **Internal Revenue Service (IRS)**—Information on canceled debts, foreclosures, repossessions, and abandonments. IRS publication 4681 discusses your income tax obligation if you negotiated a settlement on a debt. Chapter 2, page 12, example 2 gives an example of automobile repossession. See https://www.irs.gov/pub/irs-pdf/p4681.pdf.

- **The National Association of Consumer Advocates**—An association of consumer attorneys who can advise you if you are having problems with CRAs or collection agencies. See http://www.consumeradvocates.org/for-consumers/credit-reporting.

- **Student Loan Repayment**—Guide to repaying federal student loans. Excellent resource to get help if you are having problems making your payments. https://studentaid.ed.gov/sa/repay-loans.

- **Statute of Limitations**—Chart showing how much time a debt collector has to bring a lawsuit against you in court in all fifty states. http://www.bankrate.com/finance/credit-cards/state-statutes-of-limitations-for-old-debts-1.aspx.

- **Better Money Habits**—Video by Bank of America in partnership with the Khan Academy on options for people who don't like to budget. https://bettermoneyhabits.bankofamerica.com/en/saving-budgeting/how-to-money-management-better.

RECOMMENDED BOOKS

Bucci, Steve. *Credit Repair Kit for Dummies*, 4th ed.

Leonard, Robin. *Credit Repair: Make a Plan, Improve Your Credit, Avoid Scams.* 12th ed. 2015.

National Consumer Law Center. *Guide to Surviving Debt.* 10th ed. 2016.

Exhibits

Make a Budget

Use this worksheet to see how much money you spend this month. Then, use this month's information to help you plan next month's budget.

Some bills are monthly and some come less often. If you have an expense that does not occur every month, put it in the "Other expenses this month" category.

MONTH _____ YEAR _____

My income this month

Income	Monthly total
Paychecks (salary after taxes, benefits, and check cashing fees)	$
Other income (after taxes) for example: child support	$
Total monthly income	$

Income

My expenses this month

	Expenses	Monthly total
HOUSING	Rent or mortgage	$
	Renter's insurance or homeowner's insurance	$
	Utilities (like electricity and gas)	$
	Internet, cable, and phones	$
	Other housing expenses (like property taxes)	$

	Expenses	Monthly total
FOOD	Groceries and household supplies	$
	Meals out	$
	Other food expenses	$

	Expenses	Monthly total
TRANSPORTATION	Public transportation and taxis	$
	Gas for car	$
	Parking and tolls	$
	Car maintenance (like oil changes)	$
	Car insurance	$
	Car loan	$
	Other transportation expenses	$

Make a Budget

	Expenses	Monthly total
HEALTH	Medicine	$
	Health insurance	$
	Other health expenses (like doctors' appointments and eyeglasses)	$
PERSONAL AND FAMILY	Child care	$
	Child support	$
	Money given or sent to family	$
	Clothing and shoes	$
	Laundry	$
	Donations	$
	Entertainment (like movies and amusement parks)	$
	Other personal or family expenses (like beauty care)	$
FINANCE	Fees for cashier's checks and money transfers	$
	Prepaid cards and phone cards	$
	Bank or credit card fees	$
	Other fees	$
OTHER	School costs (like supplies, tuition, student loans)	$
	Other payments (like credit credit cards and savings)	$
	Other expenses this month	$
	Total monthly expenses	$

Expenses

$ [_____] — $ [_____] = $ [_____]

Income   Expenses

Maybe your income is more than your expenses. You have money left to save or spend.

Maybe your expenses are more than your income. Look at your budget to find expenses to cut.

September 2012 | Federal Trade Commission | consumer.gov

Annual Credit Report Request Form

You have the right to get a free copy of your credit file disclosure, commonly called a credit report, once every 12 months, from each of the nationwide consumer credit reporting companies, Equifax, Experian and TransUnion.

For instant access to your free credit report, visit www.annualcreditreport.com.

For more information on obtaining your free credit report, visit www.annualcreditreport.com or call 877-322-8228.

Use this form if you prefer to write to request your credit report from any, or all, of the nationwide consumer credit reporting companies. The following information is required to process your request. **Omission of any information may delay your request.**

Once complete, fold (do not staple or tape), place into a #10 envelope, affix required postage and mail to:
Annual Credit Report Request Service P.O. Box 105281 Atlanta, GA 30348-5281.

Please use a Black or Blue Pen and write your responses in PRINTED CAPITAL LETTERS without touching the sides of the boxes like the examples listed below:

`3 S C 7 E F G H I J K L M N O P Q R S T U V W X Y Z`   `0 1 2 3 4 5 6 7 8 9`

Social Security Number:

☐☐☐ - ☐☐ - ☐☐☐☐

Date of Birth:

☐☐ / ☐☐ / ☐☐☐☐

Month Day Year

Fold Here   *Fold Here*

First Name   M.I.

Last Name   JR, SR, III, etc.

Current Mailing Address:

House Number   Street Name

Apartment Number / Private Mailbox   For Puerto Rico Only: Print Urbanization Name

City   State   ZipCode

Previous Mailing Address (complete only if at current mailing address for less than two years):

House Number   Street Name

Fold Here   *Fold Here*

Apartment Number / Private Mailbox   For Puerto Rico Only: Print Urbanization Name

City   State   ZipCode

Shade Circle Like This → ●

Not Like This → ☒ ☑

I want a credit report from (shade each that you would like to receive):
○ Equifax
○ Experian
○ TransUnion

○ Shade here if, for security reasons, you want your credit report to include no more than the last four digits of your Social Security Number.

If additional information is needed to process your request, the consumer credit reporting company will contact you by mail.

Your request will be processed within 15 days of receipt and then mailed to you.

Copyright 2017, Central Source LLC

31238

Credit Score Flowchart

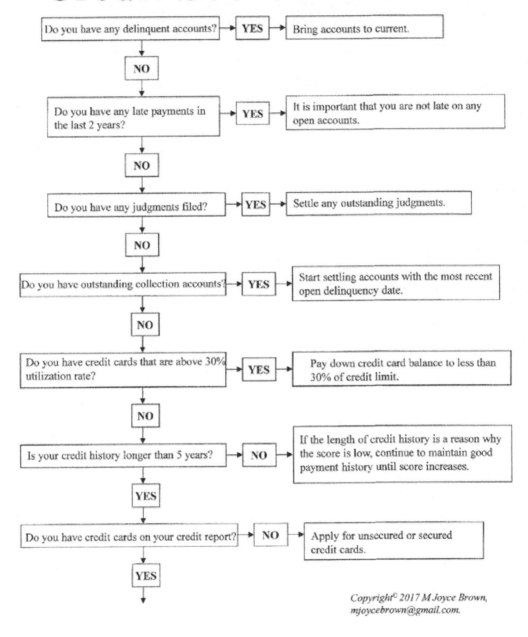

Do you have any delinquent accounts? → **YES** → Bring accounts to current.

↓ **NO**

Do you have any late payments in the last 2 years? → **YES** → It is important that you are not late on any open accounts.

↓ **NO**

Do you have any judgments filed? → **YES** → Settle any outstanding judgments.

↓ **NO**

Do you have outstanding collection accounts? → **YES** → Start settling accounts with the most recent open delinquency date.

↓ **NO**

Do you have credit cards that are above 30% utilization rate? → **YES** → Pay down credit card balance to less than 30% of credit limit.

↓ **NO**

Is your credit history longer than 5 years? → **NO** → If the length of credit history is a reason why the score is low, continue to maintain good payment history until score increases.

↓ **YES**

Do you have credit cards on your credit report? → **NO** → Apply for unsecured or secured credit cards.

↓ **YES**

Copyright© 2017 M Joyce Brown, mjoycebrown@gmail.com.

Credit Score Flowchart

Page 2

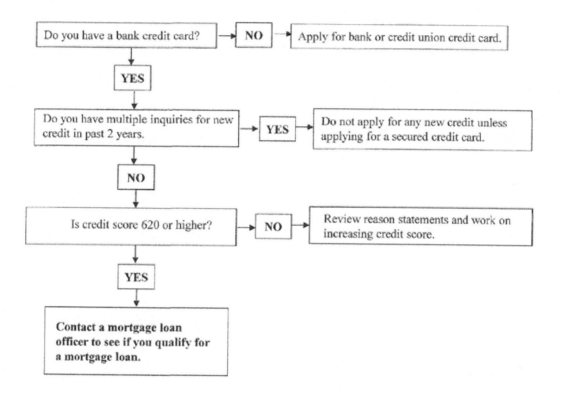

Credit Repair Flowchart

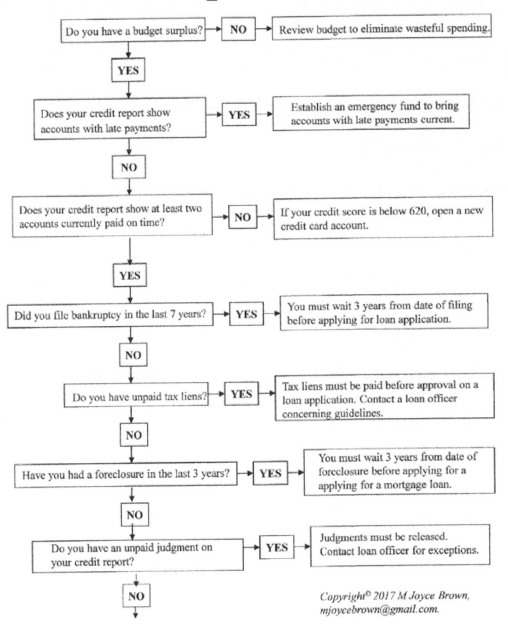

Copyright© 2017 M Joyce Brown,
mjoycebrown@gmail.com.

Credit Repair Flowchart

Page 2

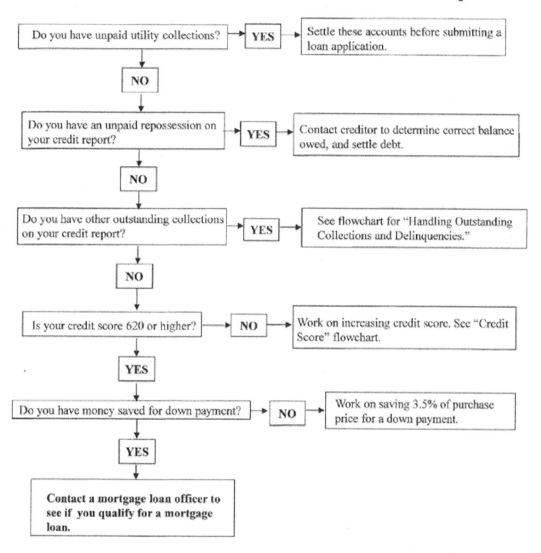

Handling Outstanding Collections and Delinquencies

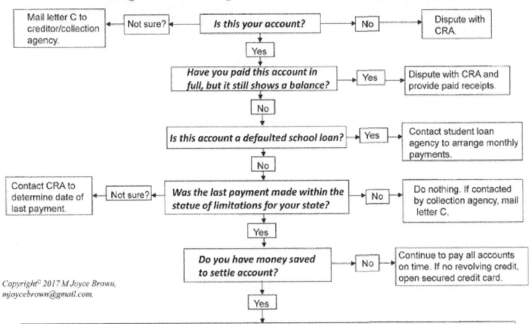

Copyright© 2017 M Joyce Brown,
mjoycebrown@gmail.com.

Negotiate settlement for deletion or positive statement using Expert Credit Repair's debt settlement script. If the creditor does not delete or provide a positive statement, make a note to call at another time and move to next account. Repeat process until you have attempted to negotiate a settlement on all outstanding collections and delinquencies on your credit report.

Credit Bureau Dispute Form

If there are inaccuracies on your credit file, you need to contact the credit reporting agency (CRA's) reporting the wrong data. Please complete and send a form to each of the CRA's with two forms of ID: (1) government issued ID card (such as driver's license, or a state, or Military ID or passport) ; and one copy of utility bill, bank, or insurance statement showing the same address.
Remember to make a copy for your records.

Current Persona Info

First Name_____ Middle _____ Last_____
_____ Jr. _____ Sr. _____   Date of Birth (MM/DD/YYYY)_____/_____/_____

Address_____
City _____ State _____ Zip _____

Previous Address (if moved within the past two yers)_____
City _____ State _____ Zip _____

Telephone Number _____

Social Security Number (Necessary to Access Your Credit Reports) __ __ __ - __ __ - __ __ __ __

*Signature*_____ Date_____

Mail

Mail the entire form plus ID information via certified mail (no green card on back) to TransUnion, Equifax, or Experian to address below.

TransUnion: TransUnion®, 2 Baldwin Place, P.O. Box 2000, Chester, PA 19022
Equifax: Equifax®, P.O. Box 740256, Atlanta, GA 30374
Experian: Experian®, P.O. Box 9701, Allen, TX 75013

Incorrect Current Persona Info

Name - The following names are not my name or are spelled incorrectly. They should not appear on my credit report: _____

Addresses - The following addresses are incorrect or are outdated and should not appear on my credit report.
_____
_____
_____
_____
_____
_____
_____

Phone Numbers - The following phone numbers incorrect or are outdated and should not appear on my credit report.
(___)____-_____, (___)____-_____, (___)____-_____, (___)____-_____
(___)____-_____, (___)____-_____, (___)____-_____, (___)____-_____

Birthdate - The following birthdate is incorrect and should not appear on my credit report.
____/____/_____, ____/____/_____

Social Security Number - The following social security number is incorrect and should not appear on my credit report.
__ __ __ - __ __ - __ __ __ __
.

Exhibits

Name:_____ Social Security Number: __ __ __-__ __-__ __ __ __

Creditor Name:_____ Account Number:_____ Amount $_____
Dispute Reason(s)

☐ Not My Account   ☐ Account Status Incorrect   ☐ Late Payents Incorrect on __/____ to __/_____

☐ Paid in Full   ☐ Identity Theft   ☐ Incorrect Balance (Correct balance is $_____)

☐ Paid before Collection Status   ☐ Other (Explain)_____

Creditor Name:_____ Account Number:_____ Amount $_____
Dispute Reason(s)

☐ Not My Account   ☐ Account Status Incorrect   ☐ Late Payents Incorrect on __/____ to __/_____

☐ Paid in Full   ☐ Identity Theft   ☐ Incorrect Balance (Correct balance is $_____)

☐ Paid before Collection Status   ☐ Other (Explain)_____

Creditor Name:_____ Account Number:_____ Amount $_____
Dispute Reason(s)

☐ Not My Account   ☐ Account Status Incorrect   ☐ Late Payents Incorrect on __/____ to __/_____

☐ Paid in Full   ☐ Identity Theft   ☐ Incorrect Balance (Correct balance is $_____)

☐ Paid before Collection Status   ☐ Other (Explain)_____

Creditor Name:_____ Account Number:_____ Amount $_____
Dispute Reason(s)

☐ Not My Account   ☐ Account Status Incorrect   ☐ Late Payents Incorrect on __/____ to __/_____

☐ Paid in Full   ☐ Identity Theft   ☐ Incorrect Balance (Correct balance is $_____)

☐ Paid before Collection Status   ☐ Other (Explain)_____

Creditor Name:_____ Account Number:_____ Amount $_____
Dispute Reason(s)

☐ Not My Account   ☐ Account Status Incorrect   ☐ Late Payents Incorrect on __/____ to __/_____

☐ Paid in Full   ☐ Identity Theft   ☐ Incorrect Balance (Correct balance is $_____)

☐ Paid before Collection Status   ☐ Other (Explain)_____

Creditor Name:_____ Account Number:_____ Amount $_____
Dispute Reason(s)

☐ Not My Account   ☐ Account Status Incorrect   ☐ Late Payents Incorrect on __/____ to __/_____

☐ Paid in Full   ☐ Identity Theft   ☐ Incorrect Balance (Correct balance is $_____)

☐ Paid before Collection Status   ☐ Other (Explain)_____

Letter "C"

Date:_____

❶Company: _____
❸Address:_____
_____

Dear Sir or Madam:

My information is:
    Name: _____
    Address:_____
    _____
    SSN# _____ - _____ - _____

Account information:
    Original Creditor: _____
    ❷Account Number: _____
    ❹Amount: $_____

I *dispute* inaccurate information on my credit file maintained by your organization because:

☐ I am not the correct person ☐ The dollar amount is incorrect ☐ I have never had an account with your firm

☐ Other _____
_____

Further I demand that:

1. **Your firm ceases contacting me via phone, text, or email.** You may contact me directly in writing at:
    _____.
2. **Your firm provides proof that I owe the alleged debt stated above.**
3. **That your firm clearly states its relationship with the original creditor.** If your firm purchased this debt, please provide a statement and affidavit to that fact.
4. **That your firm no longer reviews my credit report.** I hereby revoke permission for your firm to review my credit report.

If you cannot comply with my demands and furnish proof that I have opened the account and made charges to that account, **remove the negative information you are reporting the credit reporting agencies.**

Sincerely,

_____

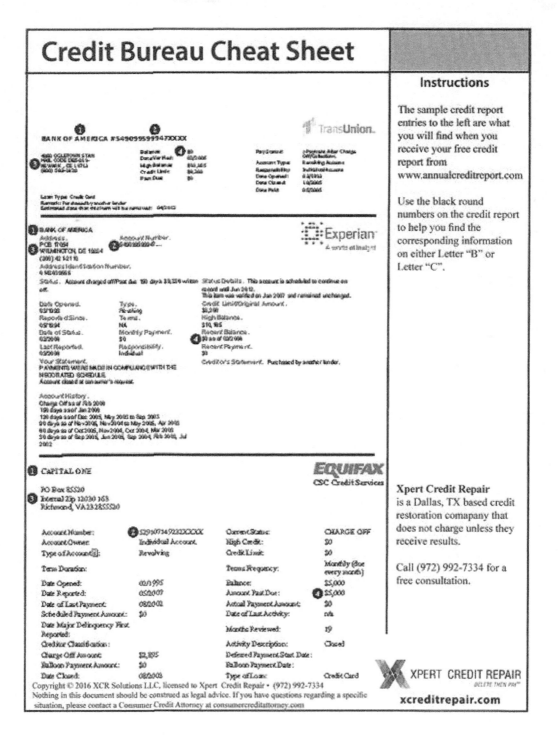

Disputing with the Creditor / Collection Agency - Letter "C"

1) Review the credit report for the information you want to dispute.

2) Fill out Letter "C"
- You will need to write in your:
  - a) Full Name
  - b) Current Address
  - c) Social Security Number

- From the credit report, you will need to write in the disputed information. To make this job easier we have attached the "Credit Bureau Cheat Sheet." You will need to match the numbers listed on the "Credit Bureau Cheat Sheet" with the numbers on Letter "C".
  You will need to write in the creditor's:
  - a) Creditor Name ❶
  - b) Account Number ❷
  - c) Creditor Address ❸
  - c) Amount in dispute ❹

4) Insert copies of proof if you have any. Proof can be letters and copies of the front and back of a cashed check showing that you paid an item or that it was resolved or letters from the original creditor saying that the issue was resolved.

5) Mail the envelope via Certified Mail via the US Postal Service.

 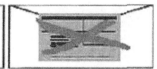

6) Save copies of forms and receipts in safe place.

7) Follow up 7 days after mailing to make sure creditor received the certified mail. Go to www.usps.gov to track the letter using the Certified Mail number on your receipt. Print out copy of proof of delivery. You may also call 800-ASK-USPS

8) Wait 30-45 days for response from the credit / collection agency.

XPERT CREDIT REPAIR
DELETE THEM PAY™
xcreditrepair.com

Debt Settlement Script

use this form to help settle debts with creditors

Provided by

XPERT CREDIT REPAIR
DELETE THEN PAY™
© XCR Enterprises, Inc. Licensed for use by above.

when you receive your settlement offer

If a debt is yours:
- Settle it with the creditor.
- Negotiate the amount.
- How it will appear.
- Payment terms.

Seven Factors that value a debt:
1) Age
2) Collection stage
3) Fee structure
4) Amount owed
5) The economy
6) The payment terms
7) How it will report

Negotiating settlement amount:
- Start at 10% of the debt owed.
- Terms
- Form of payment-
- How it will appear on credit report.
- Mutual release term.
- Get agreement in writing

TIPS
If collector won't work with you hang up.
- Call back until you get one who will.
- Do not pay without offer in writing.
- Keep copies of the offer, and cashed check.

Paying the for the settlement

After you have reviewed the settlement offer and agree with its terms, you will need to send a payment to the creditor to in accordance with your agreement.

Usually you can make payment via check, money order, or cashiers check, or **online**. When sending payment via mail, send via traceable mail. This can best be done by Certified Mail.

When you write your check make sure that you write the account number in the memo line. You will also want to turn the check over and write on back "Accord and Satisfaction, Paid in full for Acct # / Your Name."

CHECK OR CASHIERS CHECK

PAY TO
ORDER OF   ABC CREDITOR

Sum of: ** One thousand dollars and no/100 **

Memo For Acct# 122-7578   Signature
                                  Not a Valid Check

ACCORD AND SATISFACTION
Payment in Full for
Acct # 122-7578 / Your Name

Sample

After two weeks, you will need to go to your bank or money order furnisher and get a copy of the front and back of the check, money order, or cashiers check. Save the agreement and the front and back of the check for your records.

when you receive your settlement offer

When you receive your written settlement offer from a creditor what you are looking for on the statement is:

1) the words "release", "paid in full", "accord and satifaction" or "no future obligations". If your release does not contain any of these key words there may be a problem.

2) Make sure that the settlement amount is clearly stated.

3) That it clearly states how it will appear on the credit report.

Action Log This is where you keep records of what is going on with this creditor.

date	time	notes

Acknowledgments

I would like to thank the following for the tips they provided to improve the quality of my book.

My technical team: Ruth Ann Cummings, FHA, and conventional underwriter; Demi Sherman, divisional onboarding and integration manager with Caliber Loans; Joan Sledge, Realtor with Standfield Realtors and former Section 8 homeownership caseworker; and Liz Head, credit repair consultant and former mortgage loan officer.

Chris Ebert, paralegal and credit repair specialist, who allowed me to include in my book the forms he created for the Dallas County do-it-yourself credit class.

Tanya Roberson, who gave me the inspiration for the book cover.

My niece, Michaela Chatman, who encouraged me to write the book "for the people."

My sister, Leawanda Johnson, for helping me with the marketing of my book.

Patricia Rauls, my best friend, who knew nothing about credit repair. After reading the first draft, she told me she felt empowered and made me excited to continue working on the book.

I thank God for giving me the knowledge and experience that allowed me to write this book.

49025057R00060